The Scary Best of

My Haunted Life Too

Edited by

G. Michael Vasey

Text copyright: G. Michael Vasey

All rights reserved. Except for brief quotations in critical articles or reviews, no part of this book may be reproduced in any manner without prior written permission from the editor.

The rights of G. Michael Vasey as editor have been asserted in accordance with the Copyright Designs and Patents Act 1988.

Cover photo by © G. Michael Vasey

Copyright ©2019 G. Michael Vasey
All rights reserved

Table of Contents

BLACK-EYED KIDS 7

THE STANLEY HOTEL 8
   MY STORY 9
   EXPERIENCE #1: A TROLLEY BY THE DOOR 9
   EXPERIENCE #2: A BIG BANG THAT WOKE UP OTHER VISITORS... 9
   A STRANGE DISCOVERY THE NEXT MORNING 10
   OTHER GUESTS WHO SAY THEY HEARD A LOUD BANG 10
   EXPERIENCE #3: THE CREEPY LAUGH OF A WOMAN... 11

GHOST SEX 12

BEK EPIDEMIC?... 16

THE GIRL IN THE MIRROR 22

THE WITCHES' DAUGHTER 24

SCRATCH ONE, SCRATCH TWO, SCRATCH THREE… IS THIS A DEMON?........... 25

GRANDMA'S GHOST AND THE BABYSITTER 26

THE GHOST OF GLADSTONE VILLA 28

GREEN DEMON 35

"WE WANT YOU GONE…" THE LIVING HELL OF THE THORNTON HEATH POLTERGEIST 37

THE BOY IN THE SAILOR SUIT 38

THE HAUNTED HOTEL ROOM!.. 39

THREE CREEPY TEXT MESSAGES YOU ARE GLAD YOU DIDN'T RECEIVE 40
   A TEXT FROM HELL? 40
   TEXTS FROM A POLTERGEIST 41
   I'M WATCHING YOU… 41

THE TASMANIAN HOTEL THAT USED TO BE A SCHOOL… 41

THE WHISTLING GHOST OF CALKE ABBEY 43

"I WILL KILL YOU" – MOUNTAIN ASH HOSPITAL GHOST THREATENS A GHOST HUNTER 44

MY STRANGE AND SCARY NEIGHBOR 46

THE NURSING HOME FROM HELL?... 47

BOY IN THE CLOSET 48

THE SAINTS WHO COULD BE IN TWO PLACES AT ONCE 50

HAUNTED BATHROOM? 53

THE DARK PRESENCE: A TRUE PARANORMAL ACCOUNT OF A SUBURBAN HAUNTING	**54**
UNBORN CHILD	**56**
DEMON INTRUDER?	**58**
A LIFETIME OF STRANGE EVENTS	**60**
INFANCY - CHILDHOOD	60
ADOLESCENCE	61
PARALYSIS WITH LIGHTS AND CREATURES	61
PARALYSIS WITHOUT LIGHT WITH CREATURES	62
ASSORTED BIZARRE THINGS	62
THE HOODED DEMON	**67**
PARANORMAL SEX IN HISTORY	**68**
JACK	**71**
THE DEMONIC PRESENCE THAT STALKED ME	**78**
PHIL AND THE DARK MAN	**84**
ABOUT G. MICHAEL VASEY	**87**
OTHER BOOKS	**89**
OTHER POETRY COLLECTIONS	**90**

The website - My Haunted Life Too[1] - first opened its virtual doors a few years back and subsequently it has received a steady stream of stories and experiences ever since. Some of these are probably fake, some are over the top and unbelievable, and many are so-so stories; mildly scary but run of the mill. A smaller number are just scary as hell. Possibly, that is exactly what you would expect in terms of a true ghost stories website? Of course, what is scary to one person may not scare another. Given that however, here are what I consider to be some of the scarier stories submitted by readers over the years. I do hope you enjoy them. A small number of the stories were submitted by listeners of Weird Darkness[2], an amazing paranormal podcast by Darren Marlar, with whom we partner. If you haven't heard of it, you should check it out.

My thanks to those who have submitted their stories and to those who will. Stories used in this book have been edited and may differ substantially from the version published on the website. I hope that you enjoy the book…and the website.

G. Michael Vasey
Brno, 2019

---

[1] https://www.myhauntedlifetoo.com

[2] https://www.weirddarkness.com

Black-Eyed Kids

My girlfriend has read several stories about the Black-Eyed Kids on your website. She too had an experience with the "kids" several months ago. I was away on business and she was home alone with our dog - Alex. She told me that she was reading with the TV on and our dog was asleep on her lap. All at once, our dog suddenly sat up and stared intently at the door leading to the outside. He then began growling loudly before running away into the bedroom. He had never acted like that before, so she assumed it was just another one of those weird thing that dogs do. Afterall, he often barks for no reason.

Just as she got comfortable again, the doorbell rang. She thought that it was strange that someone would want to visit at that time in the night, since most of our friends were probably home and getting ready for bed themselves. She got up and peeked through the door viewing hole but saw nothing. Shrugging her shoulders, she turned away from the door when someone again knocked very loudly. She told me that the knock was several times louder than a normal knock. It actually made the door vibrate.

She turned, opened the door and saw a boy of around twelve standing there. She asked what he wanted? There are other apartments around us, and she assumed that this child had either gotten locked out or was asking for help. She hadn't seen this boy around before.

Apparently, that's when she noticed his eyes. She said the light spilled out into the hall but that his eyes were completely black. She was frozen to the spot as the child asked to be let in. That was when the dog came out of the bedroom and lay out on the floor barking like crazy.

The boy wanted to use the phone. Adena said she was almost certainly going to say "yes," but as she stared into those black, dead eyes, she suddenly slammed the door and quickly bolted it. She said she listened for the child's footsteps to walk away but she heard nothing. After a few heart-stopping moments, she risked a look outside and the child had disappeared. She told me that she had never been so frightened in her life.

There is nothing good about these kids, or their visitations. I hope my story helps educate more people about their existence.

Submitted by Bill R.

The Stanley Hotel

While staying the night in room 217 at the Stanley Hotel in Estes Parks, Colorado, my partner and I experienced three very strange events that we will likely remember for the rest of our lives.

When you hear about the Stanley Hotel, you probably think of Stephen King's horror novel called *The Shining*, or Stanley Kubrick's horror film of the same name. However, in addition to the famous book and film, the hotel also has had a reputation for decades of reported ghost activity. Claims of paranormal activity have attracted visitors from around the world.

In 1974, famous horror writer Stephen King stayed the night in room 217. Interestingly, his stay at the Stanley had inspired him to write his famous horror novel - *The Shining*. It is also the room where many guests report unexplained events believed to be caused by the spirit of a former Stanley Hotel housekeeper named Elizabeth Wilson. She passed away in the 1950's.

My Story

Now I will share the three separate paranormal experiences that have changed my belief in ghosts. Despite being a former skeptic, I came to the Stanley with an open mind. While I've seen orbs and have had several strange experiences that I can't explain, what I experienced on Friday, May 26, 2017, was certainly the most intense and frightening experience of them all.

Experience #1: A Trolley by The Door

At approximately 8:00 p.m., my partner and I came back from a quick trip to the grocery store. Out of nowhere, we heard the sounds of what seemed to be a trolley that was outside of our door. My partner immediately walked over to the door to see if who it was. I thought to myself that perhaps it was room service, but I knew we didn't make any requests. Shockingly, my partner looked through the peephole, and there was no one in sight. Although what happened was certainly a shock to us, it wasn't enough to convince me that it was a ghost.

At around 11:00 p.m., we decided to reach out to Ms. Elizabeth Wilson (or any other ghost that may have been hanging out in our room). I figured that even if nothing were to come out of it, I can at least say "I tried." I said to Ms. Wilson: "If you are really here with us, prove it." I repeated this a couple of times. This was the last thing I had said before I finally went to bed.

Experience #2: A Big Bang That Woke Up Other Visitors

It was around 2:30 in the morning when I was woken up from a loud noise. Despite my partner being a heavy sleeper, the noise was loud enough to wake him up as well. The loud noise sounded like it came from someone who picked up a large and heavy object, and then slammed it to the floor.

Interestingly, it wasn't just my partner and I who woke up from this mysterious noise. Just a moment or two after we woke up, we heard other guests around the hotel speaking and whispering. I was so scared I asked my partner to put the television on so I could just forget about it and go back to sleep. However, he didn't want the television on. He was more interested in finding out where the noise came from, than going back to sleep.

A Strange Discovery the Next Morning

When I awoke the next morning, I saw a 20 oz. bottle of Mountain Dew on the floor. My partner's soda somehow fell to the floor in the middle of a quiet night. What's even more odd is that this bottle was loud enough to wake up not just my partner and I, but also other guests who were near our room. I don't believe it was the soda that caused the loud noise. I believe it was a ghost responding to our request to prove it really exists.

Other Guests Who Say They Heard A Loud Bang

Before we left room 217, I overheard a conversation between several people outside of our room. They were talking about hearing a loud noise late in the night. I spoke with a woman who told us she was staying in a room directly above ours. After I asked her about the loud noise, she said it woke her up around 2:30. The woman described the noise as the fall of a "large barrel." According to the woman, there was another guest in room 324 who also heard the noise.

While on our way to check-out, we ran into a young man who stayed in room 326 with his father. In addition to taking pictures of orbs that were floating outside of room 217 the previous night, he too said he was woken up from what he described as a "loud boom."

Experience #3: The Creepy Laugh of a Woman

While I thought that the extremely loud and unexplained bang was enough to convince me that there really are ghosts roaming the Earth, one more thing happened that night. At around 4:00 a.m., I woke up and realized that less than two hours after the loud bang occurred, it was completely silent in our room. My partner was sound asleep. Just a minute or two after I woke up, out of nowhere I heard the sounds of a chuckle from a woman. Interestingly, it sounded like the ghost was giggling just centimeters away from my ears.

I believe that the chuckle had probably came from Elizabeth Wilson. Although it certainly was frightening and quite creepy to me, I was extremely tired. I quickly went back to sleep.

After staying just one night in the Stanley's room 217, I went from a skeptic, to a believer in ghosts. If I ever go back to this hotel, I will likely request another room with many reports of supernatural activity. However, regardless of what room you visit at the Stanley Hotel, if you come with an open mind, you just might have a paranormal experience you will never forget.

Submitted by Kirin Johnson

Ghost Sex

I like trains and riding by train, so when an opportunity to go to Frankfurt for business presented itself, I opted to take the sleeper service in both directions rather than fly. I was looking forward to the trip and as I found my private sleeper compartment at Vienna station, I will admit to a little excitement. I had decided to try to get some sleep almost immediately the train left Vienna as arrival was at 5.25am meaning I would need to wake up about an hour earlier. I pushed the three seats away and pulled down the bed and after ordering breakfast, I got in to bed and switched off the light. For a while, I just lay there allowing myself to be gently rocked to sleep by the motion of the train.

At some point, I recall feeling as if someone was sitting on my legs and as I tried to get up to see, I realized that I could not. I could not move! I could hear the people next door talking and the sound of the train on the tracks and something getting up off my legs and moving above me. There was a feeling of rising terror especially when I saw the thing that now floated above me. It was like a whitish mist with eyes and a face of sorts. It came alongside me and peered at me. I tried to scream for help. Nothing came out. I was totally aware of everything – sounds, smells, sight, my fear – everything – but I was paralyzed and the plaything of whatever this was that was now inspecting me like a cold piece of meat. Then, as quickly as it had started, the train suddenly braked, and the jolt freed me. I watched as the mist rose up and into the luggage recess of the carriage where it seemed to be waiting. I sat up and switched on the light. It was still there. I was frightened and my heart was racing. I was also puzzled.

What had just happened?

Had it been a vivid dream?

I soon came to the conclusion it was an old hag experience or sleep paralysis and that hadn't happened to me in decades. Despite that, the thing – the entity – was real. I could still see it.

When you write ghost stories for a hobby, it takes something very scary to frighten you. I can tell you that I felt a mixture of fear and puzzlement. I started to pray and then also do some self-protection. The thing seemed to have gone and I commanded it not to bother me again. after a few minutes, I lay down again and dozed.

I awoke knowing the thing was back. Once again, I could not move nor scream, yet I could see, hear and sense everything. The thing was hovering over me and, I'll be honest here, I felt a sense of sexual excitement along with the fear. The thing was going to molest me. For a few moments, it seemed so but then it seemed to know that I was aware of it and its intentions and instead, it moved upwards and peered at me again.

I started to scream 'Help', 'Help me' but no sound emerged from my lips. I was now really scared because I was at the mercy of this thing and we both knew it and there was not a thing I could do. Imagine, laying paralyzed as an entity – perhaps even a succubus – eyed you up as its next victim. I continued to struggle though I could not move. I kept on trying to scream for help. I knew there was a call button just above my head if only I could move. The malevolence of the thing was scaring me, and I knew it was just a matter of time before it started doing whatever it planned on doing….

And then, again, I was fully awake and able to move. I sat up sweating profusely with my heart pounding. I again prayed, engaged in some self-protection and generally told it to get the hell away from me. Needless to say, I barely rested the remainder of the night and my day was one of a heavy tiredness dogged by the memory of the grayish mist-like face.

Just recently, there have been many articles in the media about people who claim to have sexual encounters with ghosts or entities known as succubae or incubi (female and male spirits accordingly). The thing that really disturbed me about my train encounter and what prompted my further interest, was the sexual feeling that I had in the encounter. I really felt as if this thing was going to rape me. I found this a terribly frightening proposition – and perhaps that is how this entity got its fear energy from me, but to actually go out and look for such an experience? You'd have to be out of your mind, right?

Well, the first thing I found in doing research was a website and associated Facebook page of a guy who teaches people how to find and develop sexual relationships with demons. He says they aren't demons at all, but rather spiritual beings that are gifting sexual experiences to humanity! He says it was the Church that turned these beings into demons. Then there is Amethyst Realm, a 27-year-old "spiritual guidance counselor," who claims to have had sex with at least 20 ghosts, and now prefers them to real life men. She recently appeared on British show, ITV This Morning , to talk about getting it on with ghosts. She told how she had an affair with a shadow man and was caught by her husband in flagrante with said ghost. It all started 12-years ago when she and her then-fiancé moved into a new house and a strange energy turned physical, touching her, which eventually led to sex. "It started as an energy, then became physical," she said. "There was pressure on my thighs and breath on my neck. I just always felt safe. I had sex with the ghost. You can feel it. It's difficult to explain. There was a weight and a weightlessness, a physical breath and stroking, and the energy as well."

Suddenly, paranormal sex is all the rage or perhaps I'm just noticing more stories due to my interest in the topics in writing this book. For example, reported at the same time as the Amethyst Realm story was another about a woman who also claims she had "amazing" sex with a ghost. Sian Jameson, 26, says she made love with a "handsome" man who she had seen in an historic painting in a fully-furnished 16th century house she had moved into after breaking up with her boyfriend of three years. "A few months after I'd moved in I woke early one morning to find a dark-haired, very good-looking young man lying next to me," she said. "He was fully clothed – in a loose white shirt, a neck scarf and old-fashioned breeches. He had a kind of shimmer to him as if he was behind a fluttering voile curtain. I told myself I was dreaming and rolled away from him. As I faced the wall I slowly realized I wasn't asleep and, suddenly, I was frozen with fear. I felt a hand on my waist, but the touch was strange – light and cool."

She said that they started to make love and that while this happened she sensed a lot about him such as that his name was Robert and that he had lived over 100 years ago. "Even when he moved on top of me, pressing down, he felt almost weightless. It was very strange, but the sex was amazing. I was totally perplexed about what had happened. In fact, I started to wonder whether it had happened at all. In the end, I told myself it was just a very vivid dream and put it to the back of my mind."

However, they made love again in the morning, then he got dressed and left the room. "I was expecting to hear his footsteps on the wooden stairs but there was no sound. I watched him through the open bedroom door and saw him kind of fade as he approached the top of the stairs. And the sex was as good – if not better – than any other sex I've had. Just don't tell my boyfriend that!" she said.

Pop singer Ke$ha also claims to have enjoyed a romp with a spirit. "I don't know his name! He was a ghost! I'm very open to it," she told The Sun newspaper. Actress Lucy Liu told Us magazine of her sexual encounter with a mysterious spirit. "I was sleeping on my futon," Liu said, "and some sort of spirit came down from God knows where and made love to me. It was sheer bliss. I felt everything. I climaxed. And then he floated away. Something came down and touched me, and now it watches over me." Singer Bobby Brown has also revealed a supernatural sexual encounter saying "One time, I woke up, and yeah, a ghost. I was being mounted by a ghost." Paranormal Activity 2 actress Natasha Blasick also claims ghost sex and described one of her sexual encounters with an unseen ghost in an interview with the British talk show, This Morning. "At first I was confused. Then I decided to relax, and it was really pleasurable, I really enjoyed it."

G. Michael Vasey

BEK Epidemic?

I recently read with interest the story that you published about two Black-Eyed kids who tried to gain entry to a ladies' home. I also had an experience with a Black-Eyed person.

Last year, I took my family on vacation to Lake Country, California. We stayed in a Motel there. It's a nice location with plenty of things for the kids to do. Everything had been going well, and we had been having a lot of fun. On our fourth night, we were in our room watching TV, when someone knocked on the door. We weren't expecting any visitors, so I elected to ignore it. The knocking continued and whatever was on the other side of the door started growling. I shouted out and told them that they had the wrong room, and that we weren't expecting anyone. The knocking ceased.

A few moments later it started again, and a voice started shouting "Let me in." It was a female voice, but it was devoid of any emotion. Then we started to hear the same thing happening up and down the corridor. Multiple voices all screaming "let me in." We were terrified at this point, wondering what was going on?

I got up and looked out of the window. Two people were walking into the building. Both looked normal until one noticed that I was standing at the window. I saw her eyes. They were completely black. In every other sense she looked normal. But I am sure both the girl who saw me, and the man she was with were Black-Eyed people.

When the commotion finally died down, I ventured out of our room and went over to the reception block. The receptionist told me that she had received no complaints and had been on duty the whole time. She had no explanation for what I was telling her. I think she thought I was insane. I just wonder what would have happened if I had opened the door? Would I be here to tell this story? We won't be going to Lake County again I can tell you that.

Submitted by Rick R

I have my own experience of these "black-eyed kids." It happened a few years ago. I have never been able to really think of a rational reason for what happened. It just happened.

I headed out to mow my lawn. In the front of the ditch of my road I have bushes and flowers neatly set up. To my bitter surprise, someone had gone by and stepped all over my roses. I was pretty upset.

The next day, I saw two kids walking down my road. Keep in mind my road has several houses, so we all know each other very well. These kids looked to be around fourteen or fifteen years old. I'd never seen these kids before in the neighborhood. I wanted to go outside and ask them if they messed with my roses, but I figured they're just kids and I'd let it slide this time.

The kids stopped walking and just stood on the road right across from my house. That's a good hundred, or so, feet away. They just stood there. I was looking out the window and they were just standing right there. I went to my room to go get my shoes and when I came out they were gone.

It was around 8 p.m. and it was starting to get dark out. My power went off and on a few times. That's never happened before. We usually have very stable electricity.

Around 8:20, I heard a deep knocking at my front door. I went over to the door, turned on my porch light and looked through the little hole on my door, but it was just pitch black, even though the light was on. I didn't know why, but I was extremely terrified. I started to put my hand on the handle, and I asked, "Who's there?"

Some kid answered, "Sorry to bother you, but we are lost and need to borrow your phone."

"I have a spare cell phone you can borrow for a few minutes," I told them. "Let me go get it and I'll come outside with you."

The kid just said, "No. You let me in right now!" And he started banging on my door. I'm not talking about just hitting it, but it was like something very big and wide was smashing against my door.

I said, "You quit that right now. I got a gun, and if you try anything I will shoot you."

The kid kept screaming, "Let me in now! You're making a mistake!"

I grabbed my gun and held it off to the side of my leg. I put my hand on the lock and unlocked the door. This is where I made my mistake. I opened the door expecting either both those kids or just one kid with a weapon or something. But these weren't little kids. Standing at my door were two people, and both looked young. But their eyes gave them away. They were pitch black.

I felt terrified again. I felt like putting my shotgun down and letting them in. I'm not sure why I felt that way. As I had the door open for those 3 or 4 seconds, the taller kid started to walk forward to come in. I kicked my door shut as hard as I could, and I locked it.

At this point, I heard them both crying and screaming in a strange distorted high-pitched way, followed by some banging on my door again. I went to check my back door, just to make sure it was still locked. Thankfully, my back door was locked and by the time I headed to my front door, they just stopped.

I loaded my shotgun and opened the door expecting these "things". But they were gone. I heard some footsteps and my neighbor was coming by. He heard some weird screams and came by to check on me. I stood there, probably looking like death with a shotgun in my hand. I let him in and told him the entire event. He told me to call the cops, but I was positive they wouldn't believe me. I never called the cops.

Submitted by Keith W.

This account of the Black-Eyed Kids is a little unusual. My experience took place several months ago, in Kansas. I have been reading the other accounts on your site and wanted to share my story here.

Looking back, the most bizarre thing about my experience was how quickly they showed up. I walked in the porch, turned around to lock it, then turned back, and there was a knock. More than anything else about this story, that freaks me out. It's not something I've seen in other accounts that I've read.

I turned around and saw them: two kids, one was in his early teens. The other looked about eleven. The older one was knocking. He looked panicked and was really pounding on the door. The younger one looked emotionless and didn't say anything.

"We *have* to use your phone!"

I felt my hand moving forward, towards the doorknob, but then I yanked it back. I don't know if I need to explain that I "wanted to help them, but also felt afraid of them," but I did. It's in all the encounters, so I'm just confirming that, yes, it happened to me too. These kids absolutely strike fear into your heart.

It's always seemed strange to me that no one who's ever encountered the Black-Eyed Kids has ever heard of them before. I had at least read a few paranormal websites, and I knew of a few of the stories people had told. I think that's why it was like reflex when I heard a request to use the phone; my eyes went to theirs, and I saw that they were solid black. And I knew what these kids were.

The older kid seemed to immediately realize what I'd seen. I've heard that they usually get mad if you see their eyes. That didn't happen this time, though. His eyes got a look of desperation.

"I swear to God I won't hurt you!" he screamed. "You can trust us."

That's something I've never seen reported before.

I ran to get my shotgun. I wasn't going to just stand there and listen to them begging to get in for the next hour.

When I came back with the gun, though, they were already gone. In their place was a young girl. Her hair was very light. I remember it as white. She wasn't trying to get in. In fact, she was looking away. I pointed the gun at her anyway.

"You get the hell out of here!"

"You don't need to do that," she said, "I don't even want to get in."

I lowered my gun involuntarily. This girl freaked me out far more than the boys did, but I was powerless to disobey her. She had power.

"There were some boys who came by and asked to come into your house. Is that correct?"

"Yes," I said. I hoped that being honest with her would get her to go away as soon as possible.

"How long ago did they leave?"

"Just now. I was going to get my gun for them, and when I came back you were here."

"Excellent, then they should still be close. Don't worry, you won't be seeing them again."

She turned to me briefly, and I caught a glimpse of her face. I looked at the eyes, expecting them to be black again. Instead, I saw they were pure white. No irises, and no pupils. Just pure, white pools in her face, that seemed to glow slightly in the darkness.

She turned and walked away, and I realized something; I believed her. I fully expected that I would've never seen those boys again.

Submitted by BI

The Girl in the Mirror

I was young when I first started seeing ghosts. The first time was when I saw a woman wearing a white dress whose hair covered her whole face. I thought that would be the first and the last time, but I was wrong. That was only the first of my many encounters.

I can feel them, and sometimes see them. But, I have never experienced talking to them (and I don't want to! That's too scary).

Anyway, this one particular experience haunts me the most. I was still in college when this happened. Our house is one of those many that survived WWII, yes it's ancient and the furniture is ancient too! I share a bed with my sister and one night while we were sleeping, I was awakened by a whisper. Someone was whispering to me! I was so scared, but I still opened my eyes and saw a woman's face near mine! I tried closing my eyes, but she whispered to me again, telling me that she wants to trade places with me! I tried to ignore her and silently prayed for this ghost to leave me alone. After some time she just disappeared. I prayed again and was able to sleep again.

The next morning, I told a friend who also has the ability to see ghosts about what happened to me the night before. She then accompanied me to our house when I went home. After doing some inspections, she found out that the ghost was from the ancient closet of my great grandmother. The woman's spirit was trapped in the mirror of that closet, and she really wanted to take over my body and to trap me in that mirror. My friend says that I was lucky she didn't succeed.

After that, we switched rooms with my aunt. And I'm relieved that the ghost didn't bother me again, although I still feel her sometimes watching me.

The Witches' Daughter

Many, many years ago, I went on a school trip to SW England. One evening during the stay, there were some girls in the hotel of as similar age who had come for the weekly disco there. I was immediately attracted to one of them and over the course of the evening, did everything I could to hook up with her. I had some success and at some time after midnight I walked her home holding hands. As we walked out of town down a dark country lane she began to become afraid and insisted that I leave her to walk the remaining half a mile or so on her own. She told me a rather strange story as we walked.

She told me that her parents were witches and of the darker variety. She told me how she was forced to take part in rituals and was extremely scared. She told me that even now, I was in danger just by her being with me. I laughed at her creepy tale but stopped short when I saw the tears in her eyes. "Go, quickly," she urged me, "before you have their attention." I have to admit that a touch of ice ran down my spine and after a quick hug, I left.

I arrived back at the hotel deeply perturbed by her story, but, as you do, I laughed it off and went to bed.

At first, I was fine. However, as I lay on the point of sleep a strange feeling came over me. As if I were being observed. Of course, I put this down to my imagination. I finally did fall asleep but had very strange dreams and awoke in the later hours of the morning covered in sweat. It was very dark. In the corner of the room, I could swear there were two bright red eyes. I shut mine tight and willed it to go away, but when I opened my eyes again, there they were. Shaking I reached for the bedside light however, it did not work! There I was in sheer darkness with a pair of red eyes staring at me from the corner of the room and a growing air of malevolence in my small room.

I was terrified. Who wouldn't be?

I began to pray silently. I invoked the forces of good to defend and protect me and more besides. The feeling of gloom and despair deepened. The eyes grew in intensity.

I prayed more feverishly shivering in what was now a very cold room.

Suddenly, the most amazing thing occurred. I saw a glow appear. Slowly it took on shape and solidity. What I saw defied any logic. It became a soldier in a bright blue uniform. It looked at me and the love emanating from his eyes was sufficient to calm me. It even smiled at me. In one movement, it raised its arm in a gesture that said 'begone' and that was it. The gloom lifted, the atmosphere turned into one of happiness, a fragrance passed through the room of roses and the first light of dawn peeked through the curtains. The eyes were gone and so was the soldier.

G. Michael Vasey

Scratch One, Scratch Two, Scratch Three... Is This A Demon?

I have lived in my current house for several years. I spend much of the day out as I work, but these events have been taking place in the evening. I haven't been able to shed any light on them but wanted to share them with you to see if anyone had any feedback.

I came home from work a few months ago, and after dinner I fell asleep. When I woke up it was about eleven in the evening. I began walking to my room, which is located at the end of the hall and as I walked, I felt a stinging sensation on my left arm. I thought something much have scratched me, but when I checked the scratch after entering my room I couldn't find any explanation for what had scratched me. I just saw three light scratch marks. A few weeks later I started feeling like there was always something waiting for me whenever I would enter my home. The air started feeling heavy and I would see shadows. Over the next few months more of these scratches started appearing on me. I wouldn't feel it, but when I would shower, I would notice three scratch marks on different parts of my body. Then about a month ago, I kept hearing this really loud banging noise coming from the hall. Whenever I tried to ignore it, it would just seem to get closer and louder.

The noise usually starts around five in the evening and ends as late as five in the morning. Two days ago, I was sitting on my computer checking my email and I hear a gravelly voice behind me growl. Last weekend, I had some friends staying over and we were in the kitchen cooking and we heard knocking on the walls of the room.

I have no idea what is going on in this house.

Gail Hamilton, Kansas

Grandma's Ghost and the Babysitter

My Grandma passed in 1967. It was a shock to all that knew her for she was only 57 years old. My Grandma was a firebrand and left behind her loving husband, three daughters and three sons. Naturally, the loss of your mother at such a young age was hard for her children. They all missed her spark and often spoke about her.

A year, or so, had passed and the family was beginning to recover after the wake of such and unexpected death. Grandma's oldest daughter Steph, who looked just like Grandma, had me and my brother to take care of, which kept her busy. Mom went out with her friends one night and had hired a local sitter to watch me and my brother. As the night went on the kids went to bed and the sitter had asked her boyfriend to come over. The next thing I knew there was a scream downstairs as someone walked in on the couple, who I presume were up to the usual "teenage" activities. The sitter started to apologize to the person she thought was our mother. An argument took place, which I thought was strange as my mother was not confrontational. I remember the intruder saying, "get your clothes on and go home, you whore." The sitter left in disarray, wasn't paid, and I went back to sleep. I thought mom had come home early.

The next morning I came downstairs with my brother to find my mother on the phone. She was talking to the sitter and asked, "why did you leave my kids all alone last night?" The sitter apparently said that she had been sent home. I'm not sure if she repeated why she was sent home. My mother looked amazed and said, "I certainly did not." My mother later told me that the sitter had said that "someone came in and told me to leave, and it certainly looked like you." I later told my mother that I had actually heard what was going on and asked what had upset her. She told me that she hadn't come home early that night. She had been out with her boyfriend at a club dancing. So... I presume Grandma came in and confronted the horny babysitter. Go figure?

The Ghost of Gladstone Villa

My family and I lived at a large property called Gladstone Villa in the former mining town of Bargoed, in the Caerphilly county borough of the South Wales valleys in the UK. From 1969 to 1978 we experienced activity that simply defied rational explanation such as lights going off and on. We witnessed electrical cables being pulled and my grandfather Bill claimed to have had a glass bottle thrown towards him as he entered the main bedroom, missing him by inches. I didn't personally see this myself, but I still recall the time he came from there with the broken bottle in his hands and he told us what happened.

There was the occasional sighting, but this was a very rare indeed, so rare that in all the nine years I was there, I never once saw it, but I did hear it many times in the bedroom. It's still worth mentioning that my mother, Caroline, saw it on at least two occasions. There were also regular footsteps heard in the main bedroom every evening. Sometimes during the day when we'd all be downstairs watching TV, one of us would turn the volume down to hear it more clearly and my grandfather Bill would point to the ceiling and say "He's by here" and "He's by there now." Trying to make out where the footsteps were coming from exactly.

There were five members of the family that were living at Gladstone villa. My maternal grandfather William Higgs, known as Bill to family and friends, a retired minor who worked at the local colliery. He was a short bald man who liked nothing more than to listen to his country and Western LP's, Johnny Cash and Glenn Campbell and so on. He also liked Westerns on TV that starred John Wayne or Clint Eastwood. My maternal grandmother was Rita Higgs, she was a short woman who was a housewife, she was completely tee total but liked a smoke. She also liked collecting garden gnomes and watching soap operas on TV.

My mother, Caroline Dexter, met my father at the local bake house in Baldwin street, she was day shift regularly and my father worked the night shift. He would stay behind to make her cup of tea and chat. They dated for three years before they got married on Monday the 1st of April 1968. The Beatles were number one with " Lady Madonna", very apt. They did not get a place of their own, but they decided to live with my grandparents at Gladstone villa, which was in Cardiff road. I was born in the 24th of August 1969 when everyone was listening to the latest number one in the charts, " Honky Tonk woman" by the Rolling Stones. It was soon after that my mother said that strange things started to happen.

I was just a baby when she said it all started off rather quietly, like small tapping here and there but nothing too noticeable, but in time, the activity gradually increased!! One time my mother said the family heard a noise like someone jumping down from the attic and onto the landing. Naturally, thinking that someone was trying to break in, they went to see what was going on. When they got there, they found nobody there, but the hatch to the attic was open. Whatever it was eventually occupied itself in the main bedroom, which incidentally was my grandparents' room. It soon made its presence felt by walking around the bedroom and the sounds of dragging could be heard.

One day, my mother went upstairs to that bedroom to get my father up for work so he could get ready for his night shift. When she got to there, she was confronted by the sight of the ironing board placed on my father's torso as he slept. When he awoke, he was astonished to find the situation he was in. He suspected my grandfather Bill was playing pranks, but in time, he knew my grandfather was not responsible for it and he told his work friends what was going on there and it got around town that Gladstone villa was haunted.

My parents separated in 1972 and my father left Gladstone villa, but it wasn't because of what was going on at Gladstone villa, it was just a breakdown of the marriage. They finally divorced in the 25 of April 1975, The British band "The Bay city Rollers" were number one in the charts with "Bye Bye Baby", again, very apt. It would've been amusing but for the fact of what was going on there. I was barely two years old so I have no memory of my father living at Gladstone villa, but he would come to see me every Saturday to take me to see my paternal grandparents and to the local cinema – great times even though the paranormal activity still continued.

As I got older, I too witnessed the activity for myself. I actually saw the poltergeist activity. I saw the electrical cables being pulled by unseen forces. I saw the lights going off and on and when my grandfather Bill would play records on the Sunday, as the family did the dinner, it would turn the music off. It took exception to the British band Slade and any religious TV shows my grandmother Rita would watch.

The local police were also involved. I remember them popping their heads into the attic, hesitating and not going in, but they suggested it was my father playing a prank on the family.

A family friend, Mrs. Ivy France, she was more of a friend to my grandmother Rita, she was very skeptical when my grandmother told her that Gladstone villa was haunted. I can still remember Ivy going into the main bedroom, looking around and saying it was vibration from the traffic outside causing it, but she was soon to change her mind when she experienced it for herself. It was then she suggested calling the local press and a medium.

The medium was John Matthews and when he came to Gladstone villa he started by asking the family questions. He then began by challenging the spirit to perform by knocking on the ceiling and sure enough it responded by knocking back at him !! At some point John went into a trance to try make contact with it but, he failed to get a name. He later confirmed the obvious that there was indeed a presence there and it was an earthbound spirit and that it had unfinished business.

A priest by the name of Graham Jones was called to Gladstone villa. He blessed the property and after a few prayers, he duly left and it was quiet for a few short months after that – no incidents, but it did return and with a vengeance and this time it decided to show itself !! One evening, my grandfather Bill, my mother Caroline and I, were watching television, my grandmother Rita was reading a book, when all of a sudden my mother just so happened to look to her left and she saw the full solid figure of a monk standing by the doorway. We did not see this as we were otherwise occupied, but she later described it in detail as a monk in typical brown habit complete with hood over the head, so she didn't see the face. It sounded very much like a 16th century Benedictine monk !

Fred Davies was a friend of my grandfather Bill, they worked together at the local colliery and he would visit most evenings. Fred was a slim man who would wear a flat cap and glasses and smoked homemade cigarettes that hung from his lips when he spoke. He would sit in his favorite chair by the open fire and talk to the family and watch TV with us. One day, Fred was with us, in his usual place by the open fire, I was quietly playing with my toys by the sideboard. It was quiet when all of a sudden there was a one very loud bang! It was so loud that Fred ducked his head and I ran to my mother for comfort. When it was quiet, we all went upstairs. My grandfather, Bill, would always be first and I would be last. When we go to that bedroom, we found nothing that could account for that noise. Fred later told us that he ducked his head as he thought it was going to come through the ceiling. Fred told us of another experience he had at Gladstone villa. My grandfather Bill liked to look out the landing window that overlooked Cardiff road and into Bargoed town center. This time Fred joined him, he said he felt something brush pass him, when he looked there was nothing there.

The most frightening experience I had was when I was alone in that particular bedroom. I made sure the light was on, it was very quiet. I was lying on the bed facing the window that overlooked Cardiff road, when I suddenly felt something heavy pounce on the bottom of the bed. I heard the bed springs go just once, and I felt the bed bounce. I didn't look straight away, but when I did there was nothing there. I went downstairs to tell my family and we all went back up. We saw distinctive paw marks on the bed, like that of an animal. I later found out that my grandfather Bill had a black Labrador dog called 'Tovy' who died before I was born.

My grandfather Bill and my mother Caroline claimed to have heard a baby crying there but as I didn't hear that at the time I took very little notice of what they said. The activity got so bad that my mother, grandmother, and I slept downstairs with the lights on. It was only my grandfather Bill who was supposedly brave enough to sleep there. It was then that he himself had yet another experience in there. He told us that he was lying on the bed when all of a sudden, he couldn't move. He couldn't even shout out to us to help him. This could well have been sleep paralysis, but he was said he heard something in the room with him.

My grandmother Rita had her own experiences, one day she went upstairs into that room to get my grandfather up, when she saw the boiler door open wide by itself. She didn't stay there to see what it was, but she rushed out of that room. Another occasion she said she had the sensation of something pulling from under her foot, like she had stepped on his gown. We had the ghost for so long that my grandmother Rita gave it a pet name. She called him Johnny and my grandfather Bill would shout out that name to provoke a reaction, but nothing would happen.

Ivy Frances son Charles got to hear about what was going on at Gladstone villa and he came along with some friends and with my family's permission, they went into the bedroom. It frightened one of his friends and to this day one of his friends still says it was a spooky place.

My mother Caroline had an operation on her to and ended up on crutches to support her. The local nurse would tend to her foot. My mother was sat on the chair when the nurse came this day and the nurse knelt down to tend her to her and she told my mother not to hold her. My mother looked at my grandmother Rita in amazement as she was not holding the nurse at all. My Mother made her own conclusions that it was Johnny the ghost that was holding her so as not for the nurse to hurt her.

The only time I heard the ghost being vocal was the time we were all in the room. One of us wanted to use the bathroom and we couldn't get in there. My grandfather Bill said "He's behind there." I heard quite distinctively the sound of Gregorian chant and that was it, nothing more.

We left in the Summer of 1978, when two local businessmen bought the property and Gladstone villa was eventually converted into a small hotel and its name changed to Reds Parc hotel. On the night before we moved, there was one final incident we experienced, as if it knew we were going and that was its way of saying goodbye. My mother, grandmother and I got ready to go to sleep. The light was still on and then we heard the door knob turning, as if someone was trying to get in. At first, I naturally suspected my grandfather Bill as he was the only one who slept upstairs in that room and we thought it may have been him playing a prank. I called out to him, but there was no answer, no laugh that would give him away. We then heard our belongings that were packed in the hallway being thrown around. The next day we asked my grandfather Bill if it was him playing a joke on us. He insisted it wasn't him and to this very day I believe him.

I had my 40th birthday at Reds Parc hotel in August 2009 for old times' sake and it was the female staff that told me about the ghost, and I told them about what happened to me there 30 years before. The staff told me of their own personal experiences, lights going off and on, the odd sighting in room five, a bride in white was seen, again as with the claims of the baby crying that made no sense to me at the time. I did a thorough research of the property and the Cardiff road area and I found out some very interesting things indeed. I found out from Bargoed library and local newspaper archives that Gladstone villa dates back to 1900 and it was named after the former British prime minister William Gladstone. I discovered the previous people that lived there. The Kimmiett family in 1924, the new married couple Michael and Evelyn Kimmiett and a son named Elvin Kimmitt. He died at the property just four-months old, according to the archives of Cardiff newspaper "The Western mail " of that year. This explained the baby my mother and grandfather heard in the bedroom !!

Mrs. Evelyn Kimmiett died in 1970, soon after I was born. Maybe this is why the activity all started. I also found that there was a monastery in Baldwin street, where my parents met and worked, and there is a property directly opposite the former Gladstone villa property in Cardiff road dating back to the 16th century. It is now a public house called 'The RAFA club" A priest hide is said to be there, but it's sealed up. This explains the monk my mother saw.

What I have said here is true, I wouldn't share this if I couldn't possibly back this up and I have used real names as I have nothing to hide and all I have said can be verified by the family of those people I mentioned. Sadly some of the people I have mentioned are no longer with us. I challenge any hardened skeptic and firm non-believer and I can assure them that they will indeed most certainly question their belief system, of this I have no doubt at all what so ever. In fact, I'm 100 % positive.

You may google this property, it is still there in Cardiff road, Bargoed, Wales UK, very near Caerphilly and Cardiff. This place needs to be thoroughly investigated and is well worth documenting. I'm quite serious about this and very sincere.

Submitted by Andrew Dexter to Weird Darkness and My Haunted Life Too.

Green Demon

The story I want to relay to you is one that I will never forget as long as I live. Let me start by giving you a bit of background. The house I grew up in was haunted and I still live there. It has gotten better, but there are still moments when I get creeped out. This story was probably the strangest one.

I was 11-years old at the time. One night while sleeping, I suddenly was awakened by a presence in the room. I awoke without opening my eyes first and was scared to do so because I knew something else was in the room with me. At the time, I was lying on my stomach with my face right at the edge of my bed. I finally got enough courage to open my eyes, but when I did I was terrified by what I saw.

No more than a few inches from my face was a miniature Greedo. For those of you who don't know who Greedo is, he was the alien from Star Wars that Hans Solo killed in the bar. My mind raced to comprehend this strange green thing before me. It stood about three feet tall and I could make out its every feature: its big globe eyes, it's little ear things and it's long snouty nose which was just inches from my face. I stared at it just long enough to try and comprehend what I was seeing and then I slammed my eyes shut. I prayed like never before for God to make it go away. I was sweating heavily and petrified with fear. Determined to get as far from this thing as possible, I ever so slowly inched myself toward the wall over the course of the next hour. I finally must have fallen back asleep because I remember having a dream that I woke up with my head now facing the wall and there were some pictures hanging crooked there. I reached up to straighten them and that's when Greedo grabbed me (in my dream).

I immediately woke up and it was still dark, and I was now facing the wall as I had dreamed. I heard my dad getting ready for work and this gave me new courage to confront Greedo, if it was still in the room. I jumped up quickly on my bed and swung around to face it. It was gone. I immediately ran into my mom's room in hysterics and told her what had happened. I refused to sleep in my room for a full month after that.

Submitted by Cliff

"We Want You Gone…" The Living Hell of the Thornton Heath Poltergeist

In the early 1970s in Thornton Heath, England, a family was tormented by poltergeist phenomena that started one August night when they were woken in the middle of the night by a blaring bedside radio that had somehow turned itself on. Not only had the radio managed to turn itself on, but it had tuned itself to a foreign-language station. This was the beginning of a string of events that lasted nearly four years, terrifying one family to breaking point.

A lampshade repeatedly was knocked to the floor by invisible hands. During the Christmas season of 1972, an ornament was hurled across the room, smashing into the husband's forehead. As one member of the family sat down, the Christmas tree started to shake violently. The New Year didn't bring any respite for the family due to footsteps in the bedroom, and one night the couple's son awoke to find an older man in clothes from the turn of the 20th century staring down threateningly at him.

The family decided to have the house blessed by the local vicar. But even after a prolonged blessing, the phenomena continued. Objects would fly through the air; extremely loud noises were heard, and the family would sometimes hear a noise that suggested some large piece of furniture had crashed to floor. When they went to investigate, nothing would be disturbed. It was becoming a living hell for the family. The poltergeist still appeared in front of family members, leaving the family in fear.

A medium who was consulted told the family that the house was haunted by a farmer by the name of Chatterton, who considered the family trespassers on his property. An investigation bore out the fact that he had indeed lived in the house in the mid-18th century. Chatterton's wife joined in, causing mayhem, and often the tenant's wife would be followed up the stairs at night by an elderly gray-haired woman wearing a pinafore and with her hair tied back in a bun. If looked at, she would disappear back into the shadows. The family even reported seeing the farmer appear on their television screens, wearing a black jacket with wide, pointed lapels, high-necked shirt and black cravat.

After the family moved out of the house, the poltergeist activity ceased, and nothing more has been reported by subsequent residents. What did this family do to incur the wrath of two former tenants of one house.

The Boy in the Sailor Suit

About 30 years ago, a friend of a friend's sister was getting married, and I somehow found myself invited to the stag. I'd never been to the house before, and as we waited for the groom to arrive; the bride's mother insisted we have a cup of tea.

We sat chatting about nothing in particular when, out of the corner of my eye, I became aware of a young boy, perhaps 7 or 8, dressed in a sailor suit go into the kitchen, and thought nothing of it.

As we sat, the boy came out of the kitchen, and stood, very politely, beside my chair. I turned and said "Hello, what is your name?" He very politely introduced himself as James, then chattered away for a couple of minutes about school, games and the cat, before announcing that he was going upstairs.

Half an hour later, as we were leaving, I shouted up the stairs, "Bye-bye, James." Our host looked startled and asked who James was. Turned out there were no children in the house, let alone one wearing a sailor suit.

I never went back…

Submitted by Alan.

The Haunted Hotel Room!

Five years ago my wife and I decided to take a weekend break. The hotel we chose was a hotel named the Barony Castle hotel on the outskirts of Peebles on the Scottish border. The hotel itself lay in acres of land surrounded by forest. While getting dressed for an evening meal. My wife was sat at the dressing table while I was standing by the bed, when suddenly the Television, which stood on the other side of the room, switched itself on. It stayed on for a few minutes then switched itself off again. It did this about three times.

Neither my wife nor I felt fazed by this, until the following morning while we were checking out. The receptionist said to us,

"Oh, I see you were in the haunted room last night."

When we told her what had happened, she said the room was haunted by a maid who had once worked at the hotel. She said that others had reported being woken up by a lady who would stand at the bottom of the bed staring at them as they slept. Others had had witnessed the TV switching on and off as we did.

We didn't at any time feel threatened in anyway, but in fact have visited the same hotel on many occasion.

The Barony castle hotel can be googled, and the story of the haunting is there for all to read.

Submitted by Keith R.

Three Creepy Text Messages You are Glad You Didn't Receive

Who needs to buy lots of expensive ghost hunting and spirit communicating kit these days? Ghosts and the dead don't need such tools. They can just text you. Here are three deeply disturbing examples of texts from ghosts.....

A Text from Hell?
After purchasing a new cell phone it began immediately receiving text messages. The owner of the phone had not even had a chance to tell anyone his number or even that he had a phone. At first, the text messages were just strings of garbled letters, but then he noticed that sometimes there really were words. A call to the number doing the texting turned out to not exist, but when a text was sent back, the texter would answer. Over time, the texts became more and more legible and appeared to originate from a man who thought he was a soldier. When asked where he was texting from, he told them only *'hell.'* The only solution to stop the texts was to switch off the phone as these text messages came thick and fast otherwise.

Texts from A Poltergeist

A poltergeist in one well-documented case used family member's phones to send text messages to other family members even when all of them had actually turned their phones off. The family members all presented their phones to prove that they were not responsible for the texts. Family members even received a text that originated from a phone in which the battery and SIM card had both been removed.

I'm Watching You....

A woman living alone in an apartment got a text one night from someone who could plainly see her. The texts even commented on her new hairdo that no one had yet seen or knew about. The number the texts were originating from didn't exist when she called it and yet, whoever it was, responded to her texts back. She actually called the police thinking that someone was in her home to be told off by the texter and told that the police wouldn't find them because 'they couldn't be seen.'

Next time you hear your text alert..... you might think twice before reading it?

The Tasmanian Hotel That Used to be A School...

The hotel looks nice enough from outside and was a long way out of the city center. It has all the amenities one expects from a 4 star.

The first thing I noticed was there was hardly any cars in the carpark and also not many guests in the hotel at all, the bar and restaurant were all empty even at breakfast time.

The hotel has a nice view of the oval, but an eerie vibe.

Believe what you like, but at 4:40am I awoke to what I thought was the sound of kids playing in the room next door; thumping a ball against the wall and laughing. Also an adult telling them to be quiet in an angry voice. I was sitting up in bed by this time and was about to open the door and ask the people next door to be quiet please. Then my bed started to shake violently. I heard the door slam and it felt like a cat was crawling over my sheets. The sheets were crumpling over my legs, but I couldn't see anything moving. I really freaked out and got up and ran to the light switch. I switched on all the lights and took a shower because I thought I might have been dreaming but I was well awake. I turned on the TV and sat until it was light enough outside to go for a walk.

At 7:30 am, after eating breakfast in the empty Buffet, I checked out.

The experience freaked me right out!!!

The history of the hotel is pretty vague but there is a brief mention of it being at one time or another a dormitory of some kind. I think it was a school at some stage.

Anyways I would not recommend this place to anyone as it scared the hell out of me. I got to the airport 3 hours early just to get away from the place. Freaky!!

A review of the hotel

The Whistling Ghost of Calke Abbey

Calke Abbey is a run-down stately home that is now owned by the National Trust in the UK. It is kept in the state that it was in when handed over to the NT and so visitors are treated to a glimpse of its former glories. It's peeling walls and overgrown gardens paint a picture of the decadence of a former period and the harsh realities of changing family fortunes. The stately home was built on the site of a former religious house – Calke Priory – but it lasted only a few years and was eventually dissolved by Henry VIII. The estate was eventually purchased by Henry Harpur in 1622 for £5,350 and it stayed in the Harpur family until the National Trust began caring for it in 1985.

The son of Sir Harry Harpur, 6th Baronet, and Lady Frances Greville of Warwick Castle, was known as the 'isolated baronet'. Sir Henry Harpur became the 7th Baronet in 1789. He withdrew from society, a characteristic which continued in the family for the next 200 years, and this rather eccentric and solitary nature has shaped the house you can still see today. Sir Vauncey Harpur-Crewe, 10th Baronet, was little seen outside the grounds of Calke Abbey. Much like his ancestors he preferred isolation. He was kind to his workers but lacked in manners when it came to his own family. His passion was for collecting stuffed animals and when he died in 1924, there were several hundred specimens in the house. By the time the NT took over the house, many of its rooms had been abandoned for decades and they have been left that way.

Visitors to the Abbey have reported a strange atmosphere of sadness and foreboding and many have reported being scared by the sounds of a tin whistle. **One account** posted to Reddit describes the whistle sound and the creepy underground tunnels as follows;

WAS IN WITH MY MUM WHO CAN BE QUITE SKEPTICAL AND THERE'S A PART THAT THEY HAVE LET RUN DOWN ON PURPOSE. IT WAS QUIET SO NO ONE ELSE WAS THERE IN THAT PART OF THE BUILDING AND ME AND ME MUM HEARD THE SOUND OF SOMEONE WHISTLING ON A TIN WHISTLE TYPE THING. THERE ARE SOME OLD KITCHENS NEAR THE END OF THE BUILDING, AND I WAS TERRIFIED AND FELT REALLY WEIRD TO THE POINT WHERE I CLUTCHED ONTO MY MUM. THERE ARE TUNNELS THERE THAT ARE VERY CREEPY, AND WE FOUND OUT LATER MONKS WERE BURIED IN THE COURTYARD NEXT TO THEM. I WAS VERY CREEPED OUT AND WALKED VERY FAST THROUGH THEM AND LOOKED BACK TO SEE A BLACK FIGURE STOOD IN A POOL OF LIGHT, WHICH MY MUM SAW TOO. VERY CREEPY.

According to the UK Haunted Locations Database, *THERE ARE MANY GHOSTS REPORTED IN THIS OLD HOUSE, INCLUDING A HOODED MONK IN THE STABLE BLOCK, AN ELDERLY MAN IN A LONG FLOWING COAT AND FOOTSTEPS IN THE OLD BREWHOUSE, AND POLTERGEIST-LIKE ACTIVITY (INCLUDING CHAIRS BEING PUT ON TABLES AND PEOPLE BEING SLAPPED AND PINCHED) IN THE CHOP HOUSE. A FIGURE HAS ALSO BEEN OBSERVED IN THE LOBBY, FOOTSTEPS, AN OLD LADY SITTING AND WATCHING VISITORS (POSSIBLY NANNY PEARCE, WHO WAS KEPT ON WELL AFTER HER DUTIES WITH THE HOUSE'S CHILDREN HAD CEASED) AND A LADY IN PERIOD DRESS WHO WAS MISTAKEN FOR AN ACTRESS.*

Very creepy place and well worth a visit…

"I will Kill You" – Mountain Ash Hospital Ghost Threatens A Ghost Hunter

Mountain Ash is a quiet Welsh mining town located near Caerphilly. The General hospital, a community hospital built partially using deductions from the Miner's salaries, was closed in around 2012 with several others in the area, to make way for a new and larger hospital. Established in 1910, the hospital served several generations of locals in the area through birth to death. These days, the site has been heavily vandalized, stripped of metal, and its slate roof to now sit abandoned and forlorn in the valley. It's only visitors these days are urban explorers and ghost hunters.

The town has had its share of paranormal activity being the site of reported live fish falling from the sky in 1841! Like many abandoned hospitals, its own derelict hospital has gained a reputation for being haunted. Residents, locals, and even ex-workers at the hospital have seen the ghost of little girl wandering around the hospital, even while it was in use. A former security guard has reported strange noises from some of buildings including screams. However, a recent ghost hunt there produced a very **scary video**.

Professional ghost hunter, Lee Smart, performed a hunt there recently capturing a strange image on video of what appears to be a person's head looking out of an upper story window. Whatever it was that was captured, quickly pulled itself back into the window when it was noticed. The team went to investigate the room and recorded an eerie and scary threat on EVP with a voice saying, "You watch your back, ha ha ha, cos I will kill you." Smart claims his name was called by the phantom presence in the room.

The security guard at the site had to move his office from inside the main building to a caravan in the grounds after he became too frightened to stay there. He reported hearing all sorts of noises including the screams of a little girl and other noises at the site. On several occasions the police were called to sweep the building because of the noises he heard but they never found anything to explain the noises.

Smart and his team also reported growling noises and the feeling of being watched as they investigated the building. However, the creepiest aspect to the whole night was being threatened by a presence who he says, seemed to want them to leave.

My Strange and Scary Neighbor

When I was younger, I lived across the street from an old dude. He must have been around eighty and he always stared at me through the window of his office, since my bedroom was the closest to his house. I was quite frightened of him and ran to my mother for help. She always said he was just being nice to me and I should not worry. It was only a year later when I noticed his skin was off color. He had big purple bags underneath his eyes, and he looked at me from his window, he never seemed to leave and never without blinking.

Every night I would wake up and look out and over at window. He was always in the same position and had gotten so pale he was nearly transparent. I was terrified so one day I decided to set it all straight by meeting him. I walked over to his little, old house and walked straight to his door and surprisingly, the door was unlocked, and I could easily push it open. As soon as I entered I felt unnaturally cold, l felt like I was being watched and I heard murmuring from the other rooms even though I was sure the old man lived alone. As I ventured deeper into the old house I heard a man's fast whisper speak to me. Because it was so fast I was unsure whether the voice said. I saw a clear figure sanding a few feet in front of me. It looked a lot liked the old man looking at me from the window. The thing that scared me the most was that he wasn't standing but hovering.

I was paralyzed in fear. I heard a loud thud coming from behind me. I was so terrified I couldn't stand still. I just ran out of the house and back across our yard. My mother didn't say a word. She just hugged me and told me that I should never go into that house again.

Submitted by Bub

The Nursing Home from Hell?

About four years ago, I was working at a nursing home. I worked night shift with three to four other people. Each night we were assigned a hall on which we did rounds every two hours and answered call lights as needed. In our down time between rounds, we usually would sit in the dining hall, which was located right in the middle.

For the first couple of months I worked there... nothing happened. I was a bit disappointed and said so one night between rounds. I'd been told detailed stories of things that had happened and was beginning to think people were doing just that, telling stories. When it was time to do rounds again that night, I moved from room to room without any trouble until I got to the very last room. I checked on the patient and was moving toward the door when the bathroom door slammed shut quite loudly. I almost jumped right out my shoes and without reopening the door ran out of the room. I went back in about half an hour later and found the bathroom door wide open again.

Call lights would turn on in rooms with no patients staying in them. We'd go to check and find the room empty. They even called in an electrician to make sure there were no faulty wires as we have to log every call light. We would hear someone walking down the hall only to find no one out of bed.

I recall one time I was in the laundry room by myself switching clothes to the dryer when I distinctly heard someone call my name. I thought it odd because it was a male voice and there were no males working that night. We would hear what sounded like large cans falling in the kitchen, yet when the cooks arrived in the morning, we would investigate only to find everything in order.

I suppose the eeriest things that happened were on one ward where all the patients were on their deathbeds were moved so they could receive care around the clock. There were cold spots in many rooms, equipment would malfunction even after being thoroughly checked out, and voices could be heard. I remember one particular night where I was assigned to the bedside of a man who eventually passed away early the next morning. I had stepped out of the room for a moment to retrieve something and when I returned I was shocked to find a woman standing at the foot of the bed. There was no possible way that she could have entered the room without me seeing her. When I questioned her as to why she was in there, she just smiled sadly at me and then disappeared before me.

I also started to notice that there would be a constant whispering, though you could never understand just what was being said. That place was alive with spirits—and I wouldn't return again. I now work elsewhere.

Submitted by Reg B

Boy in The Closet

It was in 2008. I was working for this doctor as a certified nurse's assistant and was also rooming in his home from which he had a private practice.

One day, I was painting in the living room when I heard someone crying. The doctor came RUNNING down the hall at this crying noise to see if I was ok. Later that evening, the doctor and his daughter went out to dinner. I was tired and decided that I would take a bath, but as I began to undress, I heard a lady crying. I opened the bathroom door, but no one was there. I went back into the bathroom and the same thing happened again, so I looked again and this time I saw a lady with all white hair, and she said, "you can't leave him." To be honest, I thought that maybe I was just tired and so I finished my bath and went off to bed.

That night I had a dream of a boy climbing through the window in the sitting room and he said to me in the dream that "everything was ok until he signed the paper." I told the doctor about the dream I had, and he simply ignored me and changed the subject.

Later in the week, I saw the boy again in a dream. This time the little boy came out of the closet and attacked me. I told the doctor about this and again he changed the subject.

This happened a third time later that week. I must have fell asleep and when I did, I dreamed that I saw the boy come out of the closet and he said to me "oh, you are still here?" The boy tried to put a pillow over my head, but I fought him off. I told the Doctor again what I had dreamed and again he tried to change the subject. I told him not this time and that I was leaving. He called his daughter and told her what had happened and that I was leaving. She came over and I also told her what had happened

She told me that the room I was in was once her little brothers. He had a brain thing going on and her dad had eventually pulled the plug on his life support. She showed me a picture of the boy and I thought I was going to fall out of my seat as it was the boy in the closet in my dreams. The Doctor's daughter asked me not to leave because I could 'see', and they needed my help. I told her that they needed JESUS and I left leaving my bible open.

I never want to experience anything like that again.

Submitted by Linda.

The Saints Who Could Be in Two Places at Once

Bilocation is the term often used to describe someone being in two places at the same time. Funnily enough, it is not as rare as you might think. In fact, bilocation is often something attributed to Saints and other Holy people who can earn their sainthood by being ghosts of the living.

Parawiki describes bilocation as 'Bilocation, or sometimes multilocation, is a term used to describe the ability/instances in which an individual or object is said to be, or appears to be, located in two distinct places at the same instant in time.

Bilocation is a physical, rather than spiritual, phenomenon, and a person experiencing it is supposedly able to interact with their surroundings as normal, including being able to experience sensations and to manipulate physical objects exactly as if they had arrived through natural means. This makes it distinct from Astral Projection. In most instances, bilocation is said to be involuntary and not to have been directed by the individual concerned in terms of time or space.'

Here are a few Saints of the church who have been credited with this miraculous ability. Trust me, the list is very long, and I have picked just a few illustrative examples.

St. Alphonsus Mary de Liguori – was seen in two places at once; in the pulpit preaching a sermon and at the same time taking confession. On the morning of September 21st, 1774, a companion of St. Alphonsus Mary de Liguori watched him sit in an armchair where he appeared to be lost in thought. In fact, he stayed like that for several hours – almost 24 hours. He was asked what had been wrong and he told his companion that he had been assisting Pope Clement XIV, who had just died. It took a little time for the news of the Pope's death in Rome to arrive, but he had in fact died at the very time St. Alphonsus Mary de Liguori had been seated in a trance.

St. Paul of the Cross – after seeing St Paul of the Cross aboard a ship and staying on the quay until the ship was very distant, Dr. Gherardini was surprised to see St. Paul of the Cross emerging from a room at a friend's house. He approached him and asked how it were possible that he was in the house since he had just returned from putting him on a ship and St. Paul is reputed to have replied "Be still. I came here for an act of charity", before promptly disappearing.

St. Martin de Porres – spent his entire religious life at a Monastery in Lima, Peru but was seen at different times in many other locations including Mexico, China, Japan, Africa, The Philippines, and France. One Peruvian man, for example, on meeting St. Martin, listened in astonishment to his descriptions of China, as well as various people in China also known to him as he had just returned from China. Another witness testified under oath that he had observed the Saint ministering to captives on the Barbery coast.

St. Francis of Paola – was said to have bilocated on several locations and it is recorded that once, while serving at the altar in the chapel, he was also seen by some of his monks working simultaneously at his chores in the kitchen. In his biography, another example is provided as follows. . . people who wanted to see him approached the chapel and found him so deep in prayer that they decided not to disturb him. When they returned to the street, they were surprised to see him talking to some people. They hurried back into the chapel and saw him still lost in prayer.

Padre Pio – Perhaps the best documented example is that of Padre Pio and numerous instances of bilocation have been cited including the testimony of Father Alberto, who met Padre Pio in 1917, "I saw Padre Pio standing in front of the window, looking at the mountain. He was speaking to himself. I approached him in order to kiss his hand, but he did not notice my presence and I noticed that his hand was rigid. At that time, I heard that he was clearly giving absolution and pardon to someone. After a while, Padre Pio shook like awakening from a nap. He looked at me and said; 'you are here. I did not realize it!' After some days, a telegram from Turin was delivered. Someone was thanking the superior of the convent for having sent Padre Pio to Turin to assist a dying person. I realized that the man was dying in the same moment Padre Pio was blessing him in San Giovanni Rotondo. Obviously, the superior of the convent had not sent Padre Pio to Turin, but he had bilocated there."

Here is another remarkable recounting of Padre Pio's abilities. In 1946, an American family went from Philadelphia to Saint Giovanni Rotondo in order to thank Padre Pio. In fact, their son, a bombardier plane pilot (during World War II), had been saved by Padre Pio in the sky over the Pacific Ocean. The son explained; "the airplane was flying near the airport on the island where it was going to land after it had loaded its bombs. However, the airplane was struck by a Japanese attack plane. The aircraft exploded before the rest of the crew had the chance to parachute. Only I succeeded in going out of the airplane. I don't know how I did it. I tried to open the parachute, but I didn't succeed. I would have smashed to the ground if I had not received a friar's help who had appeared in midair. He had a white beard. He took me in his arms and put me sweetly at the entrance of the base. You can imagine the astonishment inspired by my story. Nobody could believe it, but given my presence there, they had no choice. I recognized the friar who saved my life some days later while on home leave, I saw the monk in one of my mother's pictures. She told me she had asked Padre Pio to look after me."

G. Michael Vasey

Haunted Bathroom?

About twenty years ago I worked for a large company. The company had just completed a new department and I worked in that department.

One day about a year after we had moved into this new wing, I went into the restroom and as I turned the corner, I noticed the stall door closed on the middle stall. The floor under the door looked dark like someone's shadow was blocking any light. The stall doors naturally hung open, so I just assumed someone was inside the stall. I went into the first stall instead of the second, in order to maintain some privacy by keeping a stall between us.

While in my stall, I listened and didn't hear the other person make any noise. No flushing, hand washing, and no sounds of the door opening, nor a person leaving. So when I finished up and went to wash my hands, I was startled when I looked up into the mirror and saw the third stall door wide open. Not even halfway open, but it was wide open.

I finished washing my hands, using the sink right across from the stall I had used and wondered if there had been an optical illusion when I walked in that made it appear as if that third stall door was closed. So as I was leaving, I stopped to turn around and look at that stall again to see if I could recreate the image I saw previously. However, when I looked back, the third stall still looked wide open, and furthermore, it was brightly lit because the room light was getting into it.

Just as soon as I saw that, the faucet of the sink right across from that stall automatically turned on full blast. My heart felt like it stopped, and I was frozen in place, just staring at the water pouring out of the faucet! After about five seconds the faucet shut off. As soon as the water stopped, I got my composure back and I left the room as fast as I could.

Submitted by Anon.

The Dark Presence: A True Paranormal Account of a Suburban Haunting

The first day I moved into my new house was amazing. I had been living with my parents, and I had never felt better than I did to move into my own place. After the house movers had left I had some washing up to do. While doing that chore, I heard footsteps from the hallway. These steps went halfway up the stairs and stopped. I could feel the hair on the back of my neck stand to attention. I felt this sudden feeling of dread and it was really uncomfortable. I checked all four bedrooms and found nothing. The house was silent, but I still had this feeling of dread. I carried on with the washing up trying to forget about it and about half hour later. I mean, I now owned a house, right? What could be more exciting than that?

Two months later I had started getting used to the feeling of dread. I was lying on my bed with my partner. She used to stay over quite often. We were lying on my bed snuggled together.

She looked up and suddenly started shaking staring at the ceiling. When I asked her what was wrong she said she saw some kind of smoke appear in the corner of the ceiling and then a face appeared through the ceiling staring at her for a few seconds before vanishing. When I saw her face it had gone completely white. That same feeling of dread came over me like when I heard the footsteps. This feeling of dread seemed more intense. I couldn't relax at all. My partner left soon after.

I came downstairs one morning for breakfast and saw a small boy in my kitchen. This little boy was wearing dirty black shoes, gray knee length socks that where down by his ankles in a way that looked scruffy, a pair of dirty black shorts, a gray t-shirt and a gray scruffy cap and that the boy was very thin. My partner, who was staying over again, said that she had seen him too. We started to talk about what was happening, and she said that she had seen other things while staying over and asked if I had seen anything else. I told her I hadn't, but I did explain the feeling of dread to her, and I told her about the footsteps. She mentioned that soon after I'd moved in she'd gone for a cigarette by the open kitchen door which lead to the garden. After about a minute she felt someone grip her shoulder but when she turned to there was no one there as we were all in the front room. She said she always felt like someone was staring at her in the house.

After our conversation the male presence became much stronger. It was almost as though it now knew that we had noticed it. During the day the house was filled with more dread. Even if the sun was shining outside, the house would be dark. It was almost as though the presence in that house was blocking out the sunlight. On the hottest day of the year I had to have to lights on downstairs in order to read a book. At night I kept the door to my room closed and I could feel this male presence angrily walking around the house especially walking past my room. I could feel him stopping outside my room and staring at me. As if the door wasn't there, as if he knew exactly where my head was and where I was sitting. This happened every night. Some nights this male would spend the entire night just staring at me through the door. Those where the times I'd have an early night and want to go to sleep as fast as possible. When my partner stayed over, she'd go downstairs during the night to use the toilet and find the living room and kitchen lights on. Knowing that all lights had been turned off before we'd gone to bed. Sometimes just the kitchen light or the backroom light or the front room light would be on. One time the kitchen lights came on by themselves as she walked to the light switch to switch it on. Another time she went downstairs to the toilet and she screamed. I ran downstairs to find her sitting on the bottom step. She told me she opened the door to see the kitchen light flicking on and off with a huge black shape in the middle. I went to check it out, and found the light on, but no dark shape.

That male presence in the house didn't like me at all. I felt that this spirit was unable to approach me but found some pleasure in wearing me down physically. For what purpose I don't know. I've never gone back to that house. I just feel bad for that little boy. Soon after the toilet incident I moved to another house with my partner and we don't intend to go back.

Ira T

Unborn Child

When I was 12 weeks pregnant, I began to bleed, and the pregnancy ended. I was devastated.

Years later, I got pregnant again. I was about 5-months pregnant when my husband and I started hearing running sounds upstairs from my bedroom to the landing and down the stairs. We could also hear the handrail move as it was directly next to the living room where we were sat. There was never anything there when we got up and looked. This went on for a while and then baby things that I had bought went missing – toys etc.

Then one day my neighbor came over to me as I got out of my car and asked who was in the house as there were apparently children laughing and running up and down the stairs she said. This had gone on for some time she also told me. I explained that no one was home as I had just finished work. I went inside and all was quiet. I then told my neighbor that I too had heard noises many times. She said that she had got scared when she heard her son talking baby talk and found that her 1-year old son had got out of his cot and through the stair gate and gone downstairs one night. When she turned the light, on he looked as though he was holding someone's hand, but as he turned to look at her, his hand dropped to his side. She told me that she was calling a medium in to see what was going on.

She knocked on my door a few weeks later to tell me what the medium had said. The medium had told her that there were children in the house. One child belonged to her and the other one belonged to me. He asked the children their names – the boy said nothing, but the girl said she belonged to me. She said her name was Rebecca and that she was 7- years old. I went cold at this news. I ran upstairs to get my old diary and went back to the day that I had lost my baby. We worked it out and indeed that child would have been 7 and there next to it I had named her Rebecca. You see I always knew it would be a girl. Not even my husband knew that I had written this information down in my diary and when he found out, he went as white as a sheet.

The medium told my neighbor that we could ask them to leave, but as they belong with us that was our job. I just asked them to be quiet and they were.

When my son was born, the baby monitor picked up children chattering although I couldn't make out what they were saying, but it sounded as if they were playing. I heard this on a couple of occasions. Then I heard my bathroom door slam shut one day. I never heard them again after that until one day a few years back when she would have been 18 years old. I had the vacuum cleaner on and was thinking of her, which I often do, and in my mind I said, "I love you Becky" and no word of a lie, I heard "I love you too" as if she was directly behind me.

She hasn't gone. She is always here. I just hear her from time-to-time.

Submitted by Sue.

Demon Intruder?

One afternoon when I was about 10 or 11-years old, my mom and brother had left to run errands and my dad was outside working on our car. My sister and I were playing tag inside of our home. My sister tagged me while I was in the living room and she ran back into our bedroom. As I was walking back to our room where she'd ran, I heard a loud bang on the wall that's between the hallway and kitchen. This wall was not an area that could be accessed easily without moving our huge stove, refrigerator or Dutch oven, so I ran our room and slammed the door behind me. I told my sister I thought someone was in the house and we pressed ourselves against the door because we didn't have a lock on our door. We heard footsteps slowly making their way down our hallway to our room. We saw the shadow of two feet in the space between the carpet and our bedroom door, and we could hear heavy breathing then the door began to push open. My sister and I pushed back with all of our strength and we were both screaming and praying that whatever was on the other side of the door would not get in. It felt like we were struggling with the door for a while, but I imagine it was only about 30-seconds or so when everything just stopped. No more struggling with the door, no more breathing, no footsteps leaving or heavy breathing. My sister stayed up against the door while I went to the window to call my dad into the house. Keep in mind, there are only 2 entrances to our home, the front yard, where my dad was, and the back door where our super protective dog was. In addition, we lived in a very active neighborhood and this was sometime in the early afternoon where quite a few people were outside, and no one would be able to get in or out of our home without my dad, neighbors or dog stopping them.

When my dad got into the house, and we told him what happened, he was completely spooked because all of the entrances, exits and windows were locked. It appeared no one had been in or out of our home at all. He checked all the closets and cabinets in the house. He checked under all of our beds and behind all of our large furniture. He found nothing.

We don't know for sure what entity was messing with us that day, but what we do know is that spirits can get attached to items. About a week earlier my brother bought the Mortal Kombat soundtrack and it had some pretty morbid song titles, so my parents threw the soundtrack out and we didn't experience anything weird after that.

If anyone has experienced anything similar, please let me know. If it could've potentially been a friendly spirit, I would like to know how to contact it.

Submitted by Tiffany Smith

A Lifetime of Strange Events

I'm Carlos, and I live in Portugal and I'm 43 years old.

I wanted to share with you my life experiences with something that so far I cannot explain. I would like your opinion on this lifetime of occurrences.

I will be as brief as possible otherwise you will have 100-pages of episodes with experiences.

The reason I am sharing this with you is not to get a solution to my problem because there isn't one, and it's become a part of my life and routine. My wife knows about it and accepts it, my son wont probably know about it so he isn't ridiculed - but I want to share this knowledge with you and maybe you can provide me with an opinion on the matter.

I've been experiencing this since I remember I existed and since I became self-aware.

I will divide this into phases of my life as the experiences change according to the phase of my life I've lived.

Infancy - childhood

I had no idea what an alien was but sleeping for me was a terrifying experience. I have memories of me awakening and having hooded figures around my bed, some of them unhooded and bald with large heads staring at me, and I couldn't move or react. Some of times I urinated in fear in my bed - in those days I called them "snow men" because they were white like snow and had big heads the same way a snow man dummy has. Besides this, I had one interesting episode when I shared my bedroom with my sister who was also very little at that time, and one day we both woke up and the bedroom was upside down. The beds were in the wrong position, the mattresses were in the floor and the sheets were everywhere, we both woke up in the floor and not in our beds. I had crazy nightmares with miss piggy; it always had to do with she is keeping me stuck on the bed and looking at me laughing.

Adolescence

This kept going and one day I saw a program called "unsolved mysteries" with Robert Stack and they were playing Alien abductions, and when they described a gray alien it was exactly like the snow men! When I saw that I completely panicked and to this day every time I see a "grey" picture or drawing I get very frightened and my skin does that response where your hair sticks up. It's called goosebumps I think. For some reason, every time I see or speak about this I also begin tearing up and feel very sad.

While in my adolescence, I moved to my own bedroom and on a daily basis, I experienced episodes that varied in these types;

PARALYSIS WITH LIGHTS AND CREATURES

I would sleep or nap in my bed and then I would wake up not being able to move and there was a blue light with a mist. Usually, I always turned my head to the light switch and then I would be stuck, frozen, only my eyeballs moved, nothing else, even the eyelids couldn't move. I had very blurry vision because the eyelids were semi-closed and I saw shadow humanoids around my bed, doing something in me, touching me and most of the times touching my chest. I remember this could be done in a rough way or in a gentle way. One time I was really stressed while the experience happened and one of the shadows touched my head with its hand and comforted me, it patted my head. In the end, I would wake up yelling and then regain mobility with lots of sweat and nothing was there; in some episodes I was able to get to the light switch and it didn't work - like I had no power. In one episode, I was quick to get in my feet and run to the corridor that led to my parents' bedroom and I lost mobility standing up, floated and a hand grabbed me in the back and pulled me back to the bedroom while I was floating - I lost consciousness afterwards - it was too blurry to see their hands in detail but they were big hands

PARALYSIS WITHOUT LIGHT WITH CREATURES

This usually involved the same episode above but without the light. I had one interesting episode where I was in my bed turned in one side facing the clock. I had a digital clock with big red letters. I lost mobility and saw several shadows entering the bedroom and while they passed they blocked the light from the clock because they were between the bed and the clock. I felt hands in my back and then for a long time I felt them doing something in my back. While this happened, I was looking at the clock without moving and seeing the minutes pass.

ASSORTED BIZARRE THINGS

One day, my parents were disturbed that during a power outage that occurred while I was out with friends, they saw a "candle flame like light" entering their living room window, going thru a corridor and passing thru a mirror where they saw its reflection, going to my bedroom and leaving my bedroom window and then passing through the glass like it had no matter.

One day, I tried to resist one of the experiences and felt a hand grabbing my leg and throwing me into the floor - I woke up on the floor.

Another day I reacted this way - I saw the light and I knew what was going to happen and I thought out loud in my head "I am not in the mood today, piss off, go away, not today" and the light vanished, and nothing happened.

One time I had one of these episodes and after it happened, I woke up. It was winter and my window had water leaks and water entered the room via the window and wall and soaked the carpet floor near the window and I saw small footprints going from my bed to the window.

I had a particular episode in school, where we had a fence with a hole, and we would escape to the woods nearby. On the last day of school prior to Easter holidays, I remember going alone to the woods, heading to a clearing and all of the sudden I froze because I felt like something was watching me. I went into a state of complete panic and slowly limped out of the woods. Yes, limped because I had very little mobility. I was paralyzed, and when I left the woods I went back to the hole in the fence and looked back and I saw someone walking in the woods in my direction, walking not running. I could only see the legs and it had a silver suit - I ran back to school - when I met my friends it was 5 pm and they were waiting for their parents to get them but I had gone to the woods after lunch - at 2 pm and they were worried because I wasn't anywhere to be found during that time.

In my adolescence, every night I had to see if all the windows in the house were locked with my father every night as he was paranoid that someone could invade our house through the windows and hurt us.

I was diagnosed with scoliosis, an issue with the spine where you need to take correction sessions in the gym to correct it, and I was xrayed. The x-ray was a full body x-ray and the doctor that was following my case was puzzled when he saw the x-ray. I had an unknown object lodged in my leg bone, so I had another x-ray of the leg and there it was; I had a hole in the bone, and something was there - the doctor was very worried and said that I could have bone cancer. I had to do more testing and I didn't had cancer and a month later I had nothing - no hole or object.

At age 27, I moved to my first apartment.

I kept having the light and no light episodes then one day had an extremely violent episode where they were very violent and pushed me down in the bed while doing things in my body. I felt a hand on my head pushing me down into the mattress and I couldn't move. I kept yelling in my head "leave me alone, get out, stop, go away" and all of the sudden, they stop most of the hands stop touching me except the one that's on my head that stopped pushing me against the pillow and I heard my father's voice "hey son, how are you doing, are you ok? look just relax, everything is going to be ok" - and I kind of started calming down, and then I realized "hey, I don't live with you anymore, you're not my father!" - and then the hands get back and start pushing me against the pillow almost like crushing my head and I hear a very loud angry "Screech". I woke up in panic running around my house yelling out loud "help ET ET ET" - nothing was there and well, 'm sure my neighbors enjoyed the experience as well.

The next day, I went to sleep, and I see this doctor guy talking to me "hello, remember me? I was your doctor when you were a child, is all ok with you? and then his tone changes and he says - look, we need you to cooperate with us, it's very important, a lot is at stake here, can you help us??" and I say "ok I will help" I black out and I wake up paralyzed in my bed and only my eyeballs move, and slowly I gain the control of my body - first the fingers then the arms, then the legs etc.

I used to play online. One time I was with 25 people playing world of warcraft, and suddenly, my kitchen switch flips by its own initiative and the lights of the kitchen turn on, I was playing and the record for that evening was me screaming "there is someone in my kitchen help!!! to the other 24 players". Nothing was in the kitchen.

I also had for some reason the mark of a hand in my kitchen wall with 5 very long fingers near the window

I met the love of my life, and we decided to move in together, and the daily episodes became less frequent.

However, sometimes I get episodes that are very spaced out.

I started having what I call "grey contaminated dreams" which are normal dreams and all of a sudden, a grey pops up and I wake up in panic screaming.

I do remember going to my living room one morning to have my breakfast and there are 4 grays in the table. I sit with them, drink my coffee and have an amicable chat with them "sup dudes, what's up, all good?". I'm talking to them mentally and then I wake up.

I remember one time going to sleep, waking up on a metal table completely blurred, like if I was drugged, leaving the table and walking in metal corridors, and then I fall down, and someone grabs me. With the blurry vision, I see its naked, human body, and the head, it had black eyes like the greys, but the head was deformed, not pear-like, it was un-even, not symmetrical and the creature says "hello" and I say "leave me alone who are you?" and he says "I am your brother" and I wake up.

One time I had like pictures of stars shoved in my head with a voice asking, "where are we from?" The voice changed each time I would see a different star. One moment I would hear my father or my mother or my wife or my co-worker, or my boss always asking where are we? The star picture changed with each question. There were red stars, blue stars, white stars, yellow stars; and finally, I hear "we are here" and I see a yellow star and a close up on a planet orbiting. And then I hear "tau ceti". I woke up and I googled tau ceti and it is a yellow star with a goldilock zone planet (candidate to support life). I was baffled. I had heard about tau ceti; I knew it was a star system, but I had no idea the star was yellow, and it had a life bearing planet.

We had a baby. A lovely boy named Pedro and he used to sleep between me and my wife (he is a 6-year-old kid) when he was 1 month old. One night we fell asleep and when I woke up, there is a gray staring at me - at point blank range. His black eyes winked (looked like a membrane not an actual eyelid) and he just kept staring at me, and I remember thinking out loud, "not the baby, NOT the baby!" I was paralyzed but the rage got to a point where I hurled myself against him with my hands at his neck and I woke up on the floor next to the bed with a sore head because apparently I knocked my head to the wall when I pulled the stunt.

Now... is this real? I really can't say. Maybe I'm psychotic and delusional. I have a master's degree in forensic psychology so I think I would know if I was somehow delusional.

If this is real, then I don't think these creatures are hostile or have ill intent. For some reason they accompany us for our lives and for me these experiences just became somewhat normal and regular, like drinking a cup of coffee every day, having a shower, or getting a visit from our little friends; if a gray would show up in front of me in normal terms I think I would scream in panic, and then say "oh it's you" then I would introduce him to my wife and invite him for a cup of tea; that's how I'm used to this. I know this sounds bipolar but that's how ambivalent I feel about this - it's almost like Stockholm syndrome!

Submitted by Carlos

The Hooded Demon

It was 3am. I was lying in bed. My room was dark, and the only light came from the mobile phone in my hands. Then, my phone's battery died, and I couldn't see an inch in front of my face. I placed my phone on my pillow and laid down staring into the darkness. Slowly, my eyes adjusted to the darkness. It was at this point that I realized I wasn't alone. There, standing beside my bed, was a dark figure wearing a hooded cloak. I had a friend staying at my place so when I say this dark figure, I instantly laughed thinking I was the victim of a practical joke. Suddenly, the figure lunged at me hitting me in the chest. I was stunned. I'd never felt such pressure in my life. It was as if an anvil had been dropped on my chest. I thought this intruder must be holding me down with some object. I looked down at my chest to see what I was being held down with. I gasped as there was nothing touching me. Where the hands of my attacker should have been was nothing – just a space where the hands should have been then the wrists of the figure. I looked up to see the face of my assailant but all there was beneath the hood was a dark void. I realized I could see through my attacker as he was transparent like a ghost. Struggling with all my might, I tried to sit up, but it was no good, he was too strong. In my mind, I prayed to Jesus to help me. Again, I tried to sit up. With all my might, I pushed, and I sat up and swung a punch at my attacker as hard as I could. My first was a centimeter from his face and – poof – he turned into a puff of black smoke and my fist went straight through him and he disappeared. I jumped from my bed and hit the light switch, but the hooded demon was gone.

Submitted by Brownie

Paranormal Sex in History

A novelist called Robert Moss has described the experience of being visited by a horrific hag which transforms into a beautiful woman. Moss remembers how, as a teenager, a horrible hag-like creature with many arms and floppy, withered breasts entered his room and attacked him. He lay paralyzed as the entity moved up the bed, stood on his chest, and then lowered herself onto him. Moss explains how,

"Despite my disgust, I am aroused and now she is riding me. Her teeth are like daggers. My chest is spattered by blood and foulness from the rotting heads. There is nothing for me to do but stay with this. I tell myself I will survive. At last, the act is done. Satisfied, the nightmare hag transforms into a beautiful young woman. She smells like jasmine, like sandalwood. She takes me by the hand to a forest shrine. I forget about the body I have left frozen in the bed."

Not everyone who experiences the Old Hag is happy to put it down to sleep paralysis. Like me, they notice some unavoidable discrepancies between having a waking dream and an intrusion into their reality. This poster with the name Lucid Dreams expressed his/her doubts in a public forum as follows (edited for readability),

Sleep paralysis doesn't even begin to explain away the experience I had. I found this forum afterwards looking to see if others had had a similar experience and read up about the "Old Hag Phenomenon". A lot of the accounts were spot on, except for one thing… I was wide awake and able to move. Anybody that tries to rationalize this experience as a sleep disorder has obviously never had it happen to them. That's the problem though. People who have never had a paranormal experience won't believe in them and will try to come up with a rational explanation that is often more ridiculous than just believing in ghosts.

I was lying down downstairs in the family room about to doze off. It was really dark in the room with just a clock light and the small green light from my PC to allow some vision, once your eyes adjust. I heard my steps creak, which isn't unusual at all because I ran a dehumidifier down there, and as moisture is picked up that will happen. Only it didn't stop there. I immediately heard the next stair down creak and it no longer just sounded like creaking stairs. It sounded like something was descending them! All the hairs on the back of my neck stood up, and I just had the feeling that I wasn't alone. I was WIDE awake at this point, and not paralyzed, for the record. I looked in that direction and saw what looked like a black glob, a form without any general shape. It was jet black, so black that it even stood out in a very dark room. This form wasn't moving like a person in motion would, it was "orbing", like it would be at one spot one instant, then at another. It went from the middle of my stairs, to the bottom, and then was in front of a coat rack in the corner of my room, and then right at my feet. I'm still not 100% convinced that my eyes aren't just playing tricks with me at this point, so I'm not completely terrified… yet. And then it happened.

I saw what looked like an angry old person hovering above me. I couldn't tell if it was male or female, but it looked very old, wrinkled, and had scraggly wavy hair. There were hands with long, sharp nails extended towards me. All I could see was a head and hands, nothing else. It wasn't a solid figure, it looked more like what a mirage is described as. I cannot reiterate enough how angry and mean the expression on this things' face looked. It looked like it wanted to scratch me. I (being fully able to move), pulled my blanket up over my head and started praying. I even made a cross over my chest with my fingers. When I looked up again… it was gone.

I quickly reached over to turn on a light, afraid of what I might see when I did, but it was a risk I was willing to take at the time. Nothing there. I haven't seen it again since, and this was several years ago now. Needless to say, I never slept down there again, and it took me about a year to start sleeping without a night light on again.

What makes this really creepy is that a friend of mine told me and my buddy a similar story many years ago, when we were kids. This kid lived right across the street from where I live now (where this happened), and a couple houses down. He told us that one time, when he woke up, he saw an old lady standing over him with long, sharp claws, and that she started screaming and scratching him. Actual physical contact! He said it scared him so badly that he passed out again. When he woke up, he at first thought he just dreamt it, until he saw the dried blood on his arms. Me and my friend didn't believe it, of course. At that time, I'd never had any paranormal experience and was one of "those people" I mentioned above. We just laughed and said, "yeah right", and he was actually upset and said something like "I don't care if you believe me or not, it happened". I certainly believed him after my experience.

Turns out that people have been witnessing these "things" damn near since the beginning of recorded history, after looking into it. You would think it would be taken more seriously. I don't know if ghosts, demons, angels, etc… exist, but I can tell you without any doubt that this Old Hag phenomenon is very real, and at least in my case, had nothing whatsoever to do with a sleeping disorder. How would all of these people just "coincidentally" happen to have the same hallucinations (hear footsteps, dark cloud, old person, long sharp nails)? It's inconceivable that that can be by chance. And not only one, but two senses failing at the same time (not just vision but hearing as well). They try to come up with "rational" explanations, that's not rational at all. It's far more rational, IMO, to believe that there are simply things we cannot explain or quantify, but they do non-the-less exist anyway.

I have to say, I totally agree…

Jack

This is Geof James, I am seventy years of age, and I live in Queensland Australia.

The following narrative is sincere and truthful. I have absolutely no reason whatsoever to make the following story up. All I can say is that it happened.

When this occurrence happened, I would have been about three-and-a-half years of age, and I have never forgotten it. This would have been in 1951 / 52.

My understanding is that this particular house came as a 'job package' with my father's employment. I still can recall some parts of the house and its general interior layout.

At this time, my parents and my sister (younger than myself), were living at 36 Canal Street, Derby. I was four years of age when we moved to Willington.

I was never brought up with "bogey-man" tales or other happenings to cause some fear or to obtain obedience from me. Therefore, I cannot say that such imaginings were put into my head, for me to invoke an "event" later.

Despite my young age, I can recall this particular evening and event. The house was somewhat large, and it had a semi-spiral staircase, with a red-colored stair-carpet on the treads and risers. At the top of this staircase was a landing, which led to the bedrooms and bathroom.

For whatever reason, I always used to ask my mother to leave the curtains open, and occasionally the window to be partly open. It was one of these "sash" type of windows that opened/closed vertically.

On the adjacent wall to the window was the door to the landing. This door was in the area of the foot of the bed and to the right of the bed. The side of the bed was across from this wall, with the bed-head on the wall behind me.

There was a small table close to the head of the bed, where I always had a tumbler of water, as often I would awaken overnight and have a drink of water…..which continues to this day
.

When in bed, and before the forthcoming event happened, I sometimes would hear, what I thought to be a voice of someone, who was speaking very softly…….something like a loud whisper. The way this voice spoke, it sounded to me as if this person was looking for someone, but in a more inquiring fashion.

Sometimes I never heard this "voice", but it always came back; even if eventually.

There was just the one word spoke, but it was repeated. This sounded to my ears to be, "Jack? Jack?" These two words would stop for a short while and then the same two words were softly repeated. This may happen three or four times and then stop; as if the person had gone away.

I had no idea as to which gender this "voice" belonged. All of this caused me no issues whatsoever, and it certainly never frightened me. It was just there, from time-to-time, after I went to bed.

The incident which I am about to relate, I can well recall. My mother put me to bed, and as per usual, the curtains were left open and the window slightly "cracked" open.

I never heard the soft-spoken words of inquiry, and so I must have fallen asleep. Later I awoke, to what sounded like two cats fighting outside (we had no pets….but there were a couple of cats that came into the small garden); and during all this screeching and wailing from these cats, there was the sound of what appeared to me as being of empty tin-cans rolling falling onto a paved surface, and then rolling along this surface.

I imagined that the cats had run into such cans and toppled these over. All of this certainly caused me no concerns. I had a drink of water and I must have gone back to sleep.

I was awoken by a lady laughing. She was in front of the bed-side table, and between the edge of my bed and the wall (where the door was located, which in turn was adjacent to the window, at the foot of my bed).

The lady was a nondescript color, being a dark-grey. However, I could see some patterns and frills on her dress. This was "bell-shaped", front and back, but more so at the back; and something that would be seen in the late 1700s to early 1800s.

Her hair was pulled backward and in the fashion of "bun" at the back of her head. She appeared to have long-sleeves on her dress, that had a lace or other frill material close to her wrists. There seemed to be something like a "frill" or a lace collar to her dress. This lady had a bracelet on her right wrist.

However, the most significant detail of this particular lady, to me, was that she was laughing, but more so, by the way, that she actually laughed. Her laughing was very loud, and it could be best described as being in the form of what is sometimes referred to as 'hysterical laughter'.

She had both her hands over her face and partly on her forehead, whilst she endlessly laughed. Throughout this laughing, she was "rocking" forward-and-back up again, from waist-level.

I do not recall if I was frightened, but even at my tender age at the time, I thought that something was amiss. I left my bed, and went into my parent's bedroom, awoke them and told them that there was a lady laughing in my room.

And that is my story of the lady at 36, Canal Street, Derby. Nothing frightening, but I would love to know if something ever went awry in the history of this house, long before we occupied it.

Very many years later (I must have been around seventeen or eighteen at the time), I learned that this house had originally been built by a person that arrived in Derby from, what is now, Belgium.
My understanding is that this person was associated with, or was, a founding member of the soft-drink manufacturer; "Burrows and Sturgess", of Derby. (That would require investigative authentication, which I have never performed).

This newly learned piece of news (at that time), made me prick my ears up, as it made me think (or I should say at least consider), was the "voice" that I sometimes heard when in my bedroom, which caused me no alarm or other concern not be saying "Jack? Jack,?", but in fact, could it have been "Jacques?" "Jacques?"; or even being the shortened form of Jacqueline in the French / Belgique dialect?

(I have wondered whether the 'person' voicing "Jack" / "Jacques", was actually looking for a "Jack" somewhere in the house, so calling out softly to get a response from "Jack", to locate that person's whereabouts).

Very many years later, I learned that my parents often heard "talking" elsewhere in the house, and persons moving about in the house, as well as furniture being shuffled about. However, there was never any evidence on inspection/investigation of any furniture that had been moved.

There were neighbors (I never knew them of course), who always had visitors and they made some noises. However these people left, and I was informed that the noises and inaudible "talking" within the house persisted on.

(My mother was somewhat concerned and rather uneasy at times about this house. Apparently, my father was not so inclined. This attitude of my father may have been related to the fact that during World War II, he served in the R.A.F. as aircrew in bombers, which could be a physically and psychological terrifying experience in itself. Consequently, he had little to no fears of "noises or "voices" emanating from elsewhere in the house. In later life, I cannot recall ever seeing or believing my father to be a fearful type of person).

I recall when in this house, and whether it was pre or post my experience of "the lady", my aunt (my mother's sister) visited us from Scotland. The only thing that I can recall was that my aunt, my younger sister and myself were in the lounge-room one night, with "Radio Luxembourg" playing loudly.

My parents had attended some function at Nottingham, and my aunt was "babysitting" my sister and myself. My aunt appeared to be rather distressed as I recall.

My parents returned home, and I can recall my father being the first to enter into the lounge-room. Both my parents were very surprised that my sister and I were still up-and-about, and also the radio playing loudly. The radio's volume was reduced, and my aunt, who was now in tears, was speaking to both my parents and all on the far side of the room. I never heard one word of this conversation.

I was told, again many years later, that my aunt was very frightened on this evening, as she heard talking outside the lounge-room, along with other noises also (the above-mentioned neighbors had since left).

Therefore to 'drown out' these noises and voices, she had greatly increased the radio's volume, and furthermore, she would not venture outside this room to put my sister and myself to bed.

I tried a number times, after learning of this incident, to get my aunt to tell me her experience of that evening. She adamantly refused to talk about it, and sadly, I never found out directly from the person concerned, what actually occurred. (Apparently, my aunt was always very frightened and alarmed about this house, after her first visit, before that mentioned episode).

We eventually left Derby and moved to the village of Willington, where my father originated. We lived at Willington until September 1962, when we moved to Stafford with my father's employment.

Many years later, the subject of "36, Canal Street" came into the conversation with one of my father's friends. My father went on to say to this friend, that the person who moved into the vacated house at 36 Canal Street, Derby when we left for Willington; once pulled my father to one side and asked him if the house was haunted?

Apparently, my father would neither confirm nor deny this. This person then told my father that he and his wife had heard all manner of noises within that house, with people talking but "their" conversations were imperceptible.

On one occasion, late one night when he returned home from work, a lady had passed this man on the stairs. This lady said something to him, but he was very tired and unsure of what she had voiced; and didn't realize this "passing on the stairs", until he was on the landing.

Furthermore and most interestingly, he told my father that his daughter, who was about six years of age, was very frightened in the house, and that she had heard someone calling out, "Jack". Furthermore, this little girl had seen a lady laughing very loudly, in her bedroom.

Submitted by Geoff James

The Demonic Presence that Stalked Me

Let me start off by saying this story is mostly true. I say mostly because memory is a tricky thing. I know what I am about to tell you happened to me. Little details here and there may be off, but for the most part this did happen to me. That's the biggest problem with repressed memories, they aren't as clear as regular ones, but they are memories none the less. They say when your mind cannot handle a traumatic event, as a defense mechanism it will forcibly forget the memory of it occurring to help you cope with day to day life. Kind of scary isn't it? Who knows what you've seen, what you been through, that your own mind decided you couldn't handle, and then buried it so far down you could never retrieve it. That could have been me, but lucky for you supernatural enthusiasts, I did something my brain couldn't account for.

One day, back in around 2008 or so, when Myspace was still a big thing, I was going through old messages and deleting them. Messaging on Myspace was more like emails than the instant message threads we are used to today. So every time you messaged someone, and they messaged back, it made a whole new thread with every message you had before it. So I would often keep the most recent thread and delete the ones leading up to it. One thread caught my eye. The threads were titled with subjects, just like emails. This particular one had a subject title I didn't remember writing. Something along the lines of "YOU WON'T BELIEVE WHAT HAPPENED TO ME." I opened the thread and read a story I had written to my friend. As I was reading it a flood a horrifying memories came back to me. I was left speechless at the fact that I could somehow forget.

So let's back up a little bit, back to when I moved into that house. I was in elementary school and made friends very quickly. Being a bit of a home body I would always invite my friends over. I began to realize by the time of late middle school, that my friends wouldn't want to come around anymore. I probably would have thought it was me if they didn't always invite me over to do stuff at their place, or public places, but never my house. Rumor around school was that my house was haunted. Friends were seeing everything from translucent women in white in my kitchen, to disembodied faces watching them as they slept, to hearing noises and seeing shadows of men in the backyard. I dismissed the rumors. After all, I lived there, I would know if it was haunted. Being a bit of a skeptic, I would brush off what they were saying as them seeing things, or maybe just flat out lying to be a part of the rumors. I have come to believe now that this was its tactic. Scare off my friends, so it could have me alone. Make me question my own sanity. Anyway, after my friends stopped coming around, it made its presence known to me.

It started small. I would hear a crash in the restroom. When I would go to investigate, all the shampoos and conditioner would be in the tub. The skeptic in me chalked it up to cats messing around. Soon, I would see small shadows following me. Now to understand how I would see them follow me you have to understand the set-up of my old home. As soon as you as walk in there was the stairs leading up to my room. Opposite to the staircase there was a huge, very tall wall. The previous owners covered this entire wall was gigantic mirrors. So when you left my room to go downstairs you could see yourself in the mirrors the entire way down. It became second nature to just watch yourself move around the house thru the mirrors. That is how I would see these small shadowy figures follow me.

I paid these things no mind as I thought it to be a trick of the eye. But the more I dismissed the weird happenings, the more intense they became. Sometimes, I would get home and my mom would say "oh? You weren't here? I was yelling at you to stop making so much noise in your room! It sounded like you were moving furniture." Of course when I would get into my room nothing would be changed. Sometimes my dad would call me out of my room to ask me who was up there with me because he would swear seeing a dark tall man walk from the bathroom upstairs into my room from the mirrors. If that wasn't creepy enough, my room gained this thick heaviness to it. Almost like the feeling of impending doom when you were in there too long. I largely ignored this feeling, being a gamer I spent most of my time in my room, as it was where my PC was. That was until one night while tidying up my room and singing. I was purposely singing song lyrics incorrect for fun, when suddenly a voice came from my mouth that wasn't my own. One that didn't even sound human. I can't remember what it sounded like exactly, but I'll never forget what it said. "I WILL KILL YOUR MOTHER." I stopped sleeping in my room after that.

After a long while of all these things happening I was beginning to think I was going crazy. Three other people lived in that house and I was the only one experiencing anything weird so regularly. It became a daily thing for me to see something fly off a shelf or hear thumping coming from my empty room. But it was only when I was alone. This went on for a while, me not telling anyone because I was sure I was mad, and that if I told anyone they would think I was a liar or insane. I confided to very few people. That's why the message I had sent on myspace was basically a miracle. It did not tell my friend of anything I have mentioned so far. It told of one single occurrence, one so terrible for me that my own mind thought it better of me to forget it altogether.

So, since I no longer felt comfortable in my own room, I had taken to sleeping on the couch. The couch sat opposite to the wall of mirrors. Above the couch there was a bar that you could access from the kitchen. I had stayed up a little too late on a school night watching TV. Knowing I would need some sleep I decided to turn off the TV and try. After a few minutes of trying to sleep, I noticed something through my eye lids. I opened my eyes, and to my surprise the bar light was on. I am very light sensitive, so I was shocked I hadn't noticed it before. I got up to go to the kitchen, where the switch to bar light was, to turn it off. I treaded lightly so not to wake up anyone at 2 or 3 am. Despite this, my foot steps were echoed by heavy thuds. Every step I made I would hear a loud thud behind me. I had my eyes glued to the mirror to see what was making the noise but there was nothing. I would step and pounding footstep would follow shortly after.

I got to the kitchen, more than a little unnerved to find that all of the light switches were down. But I was sure the bar light was on, be it just barely. There was a dimmer switch attached so the whole set up was pressure sensitive, so I pushed down the bar light switch and went back to laying down on the couch. The whole time hearing my footsteps echoed on the way back. I shut my eyes tight, scared. That's when I noticed again through my eye lids that the bar light was on. I opened my eyes in disbelief. I know I had pushed down the switch. Also I would have noticed if the light was still on as I was traveling back to the couch. I rationalized it as me pushing down the wrong switch, and me not noticing the bar light on because I was freaked out about the footsteps. So I got up again, and this time pushed all the switches down. I was damn near running and the echoed thuds hadn't ceased. But when I got back to the couch the bar light was still on. I made one last run to the kitchen and discovered the switch was somewhat slightly raised. I was so scared; I knew nothing could explain what was happening. I turned off the light and headed back to my couch. I decided to put the covers over my head and think of something else until I fell asleep.

As much as I tried, the heavy feeling that I usually only felt in my room was upon me. As much as I told myself to ignore it and go to sleep, that if I looked, I would regret it, I decided I had to know. So I peeked from the covers and looked straight up. Above me was the banister from the top of the stairs. I could swear I saw a figure, solid and the deepest black I could imagine, leaning over the banister staring down at me. It slowly retreated out of view, so I turned my head to look at it in the mirror. Even in the darkness I could clearly make out a shadowy figure walking into my room. I was freaked out for sure, but a part of me was thinking "oh, I bet it's my sister. She had to of heard the noises from earlier and is making sure I am asleep".

My sister is the motherly type, so I wouldn't put it past her. She would tell on me for anything, so I covered myself back up and tried to pretend I was already sleeping just in case she came to make sure. Moments past and even though I was convincing myself it was my sister, the feeling in the room only got worse. The heaviness only got heavier. So I decided to peek once more. Again, from directly over me, the figure was leaning over the banister looking right at me. I looked at the mirror again, and to my horror, instead of this time disappearing into my room, it started walking down my stairs. Every step it took was a loud thud. The same noise I was hearing earlier. I watched as this figure walked all the way down my stairs. I was still hoping that somehow this was my sister and that I was over reacting. So when it got to the bottom of the stairs I closed my eyes and pretended to sleep. My sister is a little clumsy, so usually she would turn on the lights, to my ire, when she would get to the living room on her way to the kitchen to get water or what have you. So I decided I would wait until the lights came on and blame her for "waking me up". I heard the thuds getting closer and closer to me from the stairs. But the lights never came on, before I knew it the footsteps were way too close to me, it would be well past the light switch by now. I heard the thuds until they were right next to me then they just stopped. A new feeling came over me. I knew I was in the presences of something. Something I could only describe as evil. It's a feeling I had felt once before when the inhuman voice came out of my mouth a few months earlier to threaten my mother. A feeling I wish never to feel again. I knew if I opened my eyes, I would see something awful. But not knowing was just as scary to me… at least that's what I had thought. Oh, was I in for a surprise.

I opened my eyes to see… nothing. At least not at first. I looked where I thought the footsteps had stopped and saw absolutely nothing. I felt relieved until I looked around and noticed in the mirror the shadowy figure was standing right next to me. I looked at where it should be in reality and nothing. I double took and looked back into the mirror and there it was. Clear as day. Watching me intently. I have no idea why I didn't scream, but somehow I didn't. I just quickly hid under the covers and started praying. That upset, what I now believe to be a demon from my research, as it started to try to grab at me thru the covers. I could feel its hands, pawing at me, tormenting me, showing me even if I couldn't see it, it could still physically touch me. I prayed and prayed. I prayed for the protection of me, my family and my house. I prayed that in the lords name the demon would be banished from my home. I prayed for what seemed like hours, but in reality was probably seconds to minutes. Then as quickly as it started, it stopped. The heaviness that plagued me was gone. This aura of tranquility fell upon me and I felt warm and comfortable. I thanked the lord, and somehow, beyond all reason drifted to sleep.

Now this is where it gets super weird. All those memories came flooding back to me but, I have no idea when I wrote that Myspace message. I would assume I repressed the memory shortly after it happened so I could sleep and cope. But at some point before that happened I had sent out that message. And after reading the message I realized that nothing had happened since then. Big or small. Whatever was tormenting me was just gone now. And I can't recall anything happening to me for the rest of my stay in that house. That's not to say that nothing has happened to me since, but those are stories for another time.

Submitted to Weird Darkness and My Haunted Life Too by Danny Rendon

Phil and the Dark Man

I have had trouble even putting this horrible event into words…until now.

I've lived in the same house for a long time. From time-to-time, we hear someone walking upstairs even when I know that no one is awake or even home. My dog barks at nothing and I promise you that it isn't something the dog heard outside. No. It's whoever or whatever is in my house.

Actually, there is more than one entity in my home. I have created a nickname for the one that I think is a younger spirit, maybe a teen. His name is Phil. Or, at least that's what I call him. He will mess with my Mom as she hears bangs and walking. I always tell her to ignore it, and it will stop. Which it does. But as soon as you speak of him, or my mother freaks out, or I'm on my phone listening to things like 'Weird Darkness'…the activity just sky rockets. Mostly, I think he just messes with me.

Recently, I was walking up the stairs and I heard my name called. It was right in my ear…as if someone whispered to me. Another time, I really did get freaked out as I had to use the bathroom so bad and he was so active that I really didn't want to move…I stayed in the same spot until I couldn't hold it anymore and then I ran to the bathroom, did my business, and ran back to my bed. Phil is also a prankster and he moves things around. I have just started a new job and had been provided with an ID badge. For the life of me, I swear I put it down, went to wash up, and when I came back it wasn't there. I searched for it for ages and eventually gave up. Later, when I came back I find the ID badge sitting right on the bed. It's not the first time I've been pranked, and it won't be the last.

The nice spirit really doesn't bother me, but whatever else is in my house – the dark-man I call him – the darker entity…that is what scares me. It scared me so badly that I blocked the experience out until now. I haven't thought about the darker spirit in a long time. I had it stored away in my head, far, far away. But then I have been listening to Weird Darkness and that has started it back up. The reason I forgot about the dark spirit is because I had blocked out an entire horrific and terrifying paranormal experience.

The cold spots in this house come and go, but with this spirit, it's not just a cold spot, it is a terrible feeling that the walls are closing in on you. Like hundreds of eyes are looking at you. As if you're about to be attacked.

I was about 13-14 (I'm now 25). I was living upstairs at the time. I can remember it so vividly now. It was very late…I can remember feeling a strange feeling – as if something was watching me. I look up and I see a shadowed-out man. Not a shadow person nor a man. It was a dark figure, but I could see his eyes and his face. The way it looked was not natural and I have never experienced so much fear in my life. And, when it noticed that I had seen him…he turned and looked at me. I was frozen in shock with my hair standing up on the back of my neck. The worst part was I felt that this spirit could really hurt me and wanted to.

I pulled the covers over my head. It took what felt like hours for me to even gather enough energy to pull that blanket over me and even longer to lay down. Finally, I lay there, afraid to move. Finding it hard to breathe just praying and hoping that it would leave. No – I feel the spirit getting closer like that feeling you get when you can see a spider slowly sliding down its web towards you. I felt the dark spirit right by my face with only the blanket separating us. I could hear it breathing right in my ear. He was breathing like he wanted to get me, as if he wanted me to be afraid. It felt like hours listening to that breathing right in my ear. I was so scared and so afraid that I couldn't even produce a scream. I was too afraid to yell for help, as if this dark spirit was preventing me from doing so. I couldn't move.

Apparently, I must have finally fallen asleep and that was it. I had not remembered this experience until just a few days ago. It was so horrific that I blocked out the memory.

Whatever that dark spirit was, it was not the same spirit that pranks my Mom and me. I don't know who or what it was. Now, I wait to see if he comes back. Luckily, now I'm not afraid. I guess Phil has kept the dark spirit away, maybe protecting me. I'm just waiting for the dark man to come back. And I'll be ready.

Submitted by Luigi Bonanno.

About G. Michael Vasey

With over 40 books in print, Gary is an established author with notable contributions in the areas of the paranormal (including several #1 best sellers in the Supernatural category), metaphysics, poetry, and business. He is also a collector of strange stories at My Haunted Life Too. In 2016, he resumed his interest in music and released an album of self-penned and self-performed songs called The Early Years that is available at all digital music stores. Since then, he has been churning out catchy songs at a rapid rate and captured the interest of a growing audience. He has recently appeared on Radio Memphis and his songs are played at several radio stations in the USA including Trend City Radio.

He was born in the city of Hull in England, and grew up in East Yorkshire, the eldest of three boys. Growing up can be extremely tough for any kid, but imagine growing up around poltergeist activity and ghosts? G. Michael Vasey had exactly that kind of childhood, experiencing ghosts, poltergeists, and other strange and scary, supernatural phenomena. In fact, he seemed to attract it, developing an interest in the occult and supernatural at an early age and he has been fascinated ever since.

His "My Haunted Life" trilogy has been highly successful–reaching number one on bestseller lists on both sides of the Atlantic. Now he is also presenting the stories of others. His book about the Black Eyed Kids is currently available on Amazon and continues to capture the morbid interest of hundreds of fans. It's a must-read for anyone with an interest in the strange happenings of the paranormal world. Then there's "The Pink Bus and Other Strange Stories from LaLa Land," a book that lifts the veil on one of the biggest mysteries in human history–the process of death, and what happens to our souls when we die. His novella – The Last Observer – won critical praise and is a twisty story about the nature of reality and magic. His most recent books have included a tour of the supernatural side of the Czech Republic, a set of Kindle shorts on topics like Poltergeists, Ghosts of the Living (bilocation) and The BEK now issued as a compilation volume, a new book of poetry, a look at the recently headlining topic of paranormal sex and, the Halloween Vault of Horror, a new collection of true paranormal stories.

He has appeared on numerous radio shows such as

* Mysterious Radio,

* Jim Harold's paranormal podcasts,

* The Knight's Pub,

* True Ghost Stories Online and

* X Radio with Rob McConnell

He has also been featured in Chat – Its Fate magazine and been interviewed by Ghost Village and Novel Ideas, amongst others. He also contributed regularly to the Westerner magazine with his 'Paranormal Corner' feature.

Whether you've heard one of G. Michael Vasey's radio appearances, or read one of his books over the shoulders of an avid reader on the bus, or whether you've simply got an interest in the paranormal and stumbled upon this page… You are going to pulled into the paranormal world of G. Michael Vasey, and you will be hooked.

You can discover much more about the supernatural at www.gmichaelvasey.com, read true scary stories at www.myhauntedlifetoo.com.

"In many ways, I have been very fortunate meeting many wonderful people and visiting a great many beautiful and interesting places in my life to date. Some of my blog articles highlight these wonderful experiences.....In the end, I am fascinated by what we are and why we are here. I am captivated by reality and what it might be. I am a firm believer in magic and the power of the mind to shape reality. That's what I write about, think about, and obsess about....."

Gary has also studied magic for many years with organizations like AMORC, CR&C, SOL and The Silent Eye. He is a second degree initiate of SOL and performed as a supervisor for the school for many years. He has written several books on magic including The Mystical Hexagram penned with Sue Vincent and The New You

Other Books

- **Motel Hell** (Kindle)
- **G. Michael Vasey's Halloween Vault of Horror** (Kindle)
- **The Seduction of the Innocents** (Kindle, audiobook and Paperback)
- **The Chilling, True Terror of the Black-Eyed Kids – A Compilation** (Paperback, Audiobook and Kindle)
- **Poltergeist – The Noisy Ghosts** (Kindle)
- **Ghosts of the Living** (Kindle)
- **Your Haunted Lives 3 – The Black Eyed Kids** (Kindle)
- **The Black Eyed Demons Are Coming** (Kindle)
- **Lord of the Elements (The Last Observer 2)** (Kindle and Paperback)
- **True Tales of Haunted Places** (Kindle)

- **The Most Haunted Country in the World – The Czech Republic** (Kindle and paperback)
- **Your Haunted Lives – Revisited** (Kindle and Audiobook)
- **The Pink Bus** (Kindle and audio book)
- **Ghosts in The Machines** *(Kindle and audiobook)*
- **How to Create Your Own Reality** *(Paperback and Kindle)*
- **God's Pretenders – Incredible Tales of Magic and Alchemy** *(Kindle and audiobook)*
- **My Haunted Life – Extreme Edition** *(Paperback, audiobook and Kindle)*
- **My Haunted Life 3** *(Kindle, audiobook and eBook)*
- **My Haunted Life Too** *(Audio book, Kindle and ebook)*
- **My Haunted Life** *(Kindle, ebook and audiobook)*
- **The Last Observer** *(Paperback, ebook and* **Kindle***)*
- **The Mystical Hexagram** *(Paperback and Kindle)*
- **Inner Journeys – Explorations of the Soul** *(Paperback and Kindle)*

Other Poetry Collections

- **Death on The Beach** *(Kindle)*
- **The Art of Science** *(Paperback and Kindle)*
- **Best Laid Plans and Other Strange Tails** *(Paperback and Kindle)*
- **Moon Whispers** *(Paperback and Kindle)*
- **Astral Messages** *(Paperback and Kindle)*
- **Poems for the Little Room** *(Paperback and Kindle)*
- **Weird Tales** *(Paperback and Kindle)*

All of G. Michael's Vasey's books can be obtained on any Amazon site and some can be found on other book sites such as Barnes & Noble, Apple and more.... He offers signed and dedicated paperbacks from his website at http://www.garymvasey.com

Printed in Great Britain
by Amazon